This book is due on the last date stamped below.
Failure to return books on the date due may result
in assessment of overdue fees.

APR 2 8 2011	MAR 2 0 REC'D	FEB 2 0 2014
MAY 0 3 REC'D	APR 1 0 2013	MAR 1 1 2014 RS
	APR 1 0 REC'D	
		MAY 2 1 2014
NOV 0 1 2012	MAY 2 2 2013	MAY 2 1 REC'D
NOV 0 1 REC'D	MAY 0 8 REC'D	
	SEP 2 4 2013	MAY 0 2 2016
DEC 2 0 2012		APR 2 0 REC'D RS
	OCT 1 5 2013	
DEC 1 9 REC'D	NOV 0 5 2013	OCT 1 4 2017 ID
	FEB 1 2 2014	NOV 0 2 2017 ID
FEB 1 9 2013	JAN 2 7 REC'D	NOV 0 2 REC'D ID
MAR 1 2 2013		
FINES	.50 per day	

D0955357

DRUGS
The Straight Facts

Heroin

DRUGS The Straight Facts

■ DRUGS
The Straight Facts

Heroin

Carmen Ferreiro

Consulting Editor
David J. Triggle, Ph.D.
School of Pharmacy and Pharmaceutical Sciences
State University of New York at Buffalo

CHELSEA HOUSE
P U B L I S H E R S
An imprint of Infobase Publishing

Heroin

Copyright © 2003 by Infobase Publishing

All rights reserved. No part of this book may be reproduced or utilized in any form or by any means, electronic or mechanical, including photocopying, recording, or by any information storage or retrieval systems, without permission in writing from the publisher. For information contact:

Chelsea House
An imprint of Infobase Publishing
132 West 31st Street
New York NY 10001

Library of Congress Cataloging-in-Publication Data

Ferreiro, Carmen.
   Heroin / by Carmen Ferreiro.
      v. cm.—(Drugs, the straight facts)
Includes bibliographical references and index.
Contents: History, properties, and effects of heroin—Long-term effects of heroin—Health effects of heroin—Trends and attitudes—Heroin addiction—Heroin and the law.
   ISBN 0-7910-7262-2
   1. Heroin habit—Juvenile literature. 2. Heroin—History—Juvenile literature. [1. Heroin habit. 2. Drug abuse.] I. Title. II. Series.
HV5822.H4 F473 2003
362.29'3—dc21
                                                                        2002155986

Chelsea House books are available at special discounts when purchased in bulk quantities for businesses, associations, institutions, or sales promotions. Please call our Special Sales Department in New York at (212) 967-8800 or (800) 322-8755.

You can find Chelsea House on the World Wide Web at
http://www.chelseahouse.com

Text and cover design by Terry Mallon

Printed in the United States of America

Lake 21C 10 9 8 7 6 5 4 3 2

This book is printed on acid-free paper.

Table of Contents

The Use and Abuse of Drugs

The issues associated with drug use and abuse in contemporary society are vexing subjects, fraught with political agendas and ideals that often obscure essential information that teens need to know to have intelligent discussions about how to best deal with the problems associated with drug use and abuse. *Drugs: The Straight Facts* aims to provide this essential information through straightforward explanations of how an individual drug or group of drugs works in both therapeutic and non-therapeutic conditions; with historical information about the use and abuse of specific drugs; with discussion of drug policies in the United States; and with an ample list of further reading.

From the start, the series uses the word *"drug"* to describe psychoactive substances that are used for medicinal or non-medicinal purposes. Included in this broad category are substances that are legal or illegal. It is worth noting that humans have used many of these substances for hundreds, if not thousands of years. For example, traces of marijuana and cocaine have been found in Egyptian mummies; the use of peyote and Amanita fungi has long been a component of religious ceremonies worldwide; and alcohol production and consumption have been an integral part of many human cultures' social and religious ceremonies. One can speculate about why early human societies chose to use such drugs. Perhaps, anything that could provide relief from the harshness of life—anything that could make the poor conditions and fatigue associated with hard work easier to bear—was considered a welcome tonic. Life was likely to be, according to the seventeenth century English philosopher Thomas Hobbes, *"poor, nasty, brutish and short."* One can also speculate about modern human societies' continued use and abuse of drugs. Whatever the reasons, the consequences of sustained drug use are not insignificant—addiction, overdose, incarceration, and drug wars—and must be dealt with by an informed citizenry.

The problem that faces our society today is how to break

the connection between our demand for drugs and the willingness of largely outside countries to supply this highly profitable trade. This is the same problem we have faced since narcotics and cocaine were outlawed by the Harrison Narcotic Act of 1914, and we have yet to defeat it despite current expenditures of approximately $20 billion per year on "the war on drugs." The first step in meeting any challenge is always an intelligent and informed citizenry. The purpose of this series is to educate our readers so that they can make informed decisions about issues related to drugs and drug abuse.

SUGGESTED ADDITIONAL READING

David T. Courtwright, *Forces of Habit. Drugs and the making of the modern world.* Cambridge, Mass.: Harvard University Press, 2001. David Courtwright is Professor of History at the University of North Florida.

Richard Davenport-Hines, *The Pursuit of Oblivion. A global history of narcotics.* New York: Norton, 2002. The author is a professional historian and a member of the Royal Historical Society.

Aldous Huxley, *Brave New World.* New York: Harper & Row, 1932. Huxley's book, written in 1932, paints a picture of a cloned society devoted to the pursuit only of happiness.

David J. Triggle, Ph.D.
University Professor
School of Pharmacy and Pharmaceutical Sciences
State University of New York at Buffalo

1

History, Properties, and Effects of Heroin

Heroin is a highly addictive drug, and its abuse has repercussions that extend far beyond the individual users. The health and social consequences of drug abuse— HIV/AIDS, violence, tuberculosis, fetal effects, crime, and disruptions in family, workplace, and educational environments—have a devastating impact on society and cost billions of dollars each year.

This is how Alan I. Leshner, director of the National Institute on Drug Abuse (NIDA) describes heroin. Yet heroin—that is, pure heroin—is just a semi-synthetic alkaloid (organic substance from plants), a diacetyl derivative of morphine, a white powder as harmless looking as powdered sugar. Street heroin, however, is an entirely different matter, and it is this form of heroin that Leshner is speaking about.

STREET HEROIN

Because heroin is illegal in the United States, it has become a black market commodity (product available illegally only) and, as such, its color, purity, and even its name have changed. On the street, heroin is called smack, horse, H, dope, skag, or junk. As in other commercial markets, the dealers give their product brand names like "Tango &

Cash," "DOA" (dead on arrival), "Body Bag" (no explanation needed), and the more subtle "Red Rum"—murder spelled backward. A "fix" (enough heroin for a single high) is usually bought in a glassine (thin transparent paper that resists air and grease) envelope with the brand name stamped on it.

Street heroin is far from pure. Every time it is traded down the distribution chain, it is "cut," which means that it is mixed with other products to increase its weight and the profit of its sale. Some of these products are innocuous—for example, sugar, starch, powered milk, quinine, brick dust, and starch. Others are intrinsically harmful—for example, the harmful poison strychnine and the potentially dangerous talcum powder, which, when injected in a vein, does not dissolve in the bloodstream but forms little particles that can cause vein blockage. Sometimes heroin is laced with other

PURITY

According to the DEA (U.S. Drug Enforcement Administration), heroin sold in the United States has increased in purity from an average of less than 4 percent in 1980 to 71 percent in 1998. Cities on the East Coast in New York, New Jersey, Maryland, and Pennsylvania are reported to have heroin of the highest purity. Bags of 94 percent pure heroin could be found in Manhattan in 1995 at the affordable price of $10.

The reasons for this shocking increase in purity are wider availability, more sophisticated processing labs, and different marketing strategy with fewer intermediaries. The involvement of the Colombian Drug Cartel in the heroin business since 1991 has helped this trend, too. Apparently, the heroin from Colombia was at first hard to adulterate because a different process was used in its synthesis. Because the first attempts to cut the drug with other substances ruined the product, the retailers decided to sell the drug as they received it.

drugs. Sometimes it is sold pure, without additives. This is even more dangerous since its potency may cause the unaware user to overdose and die. Ironically, among heroin buyers, the fact that a particular brand has caused death by overdose makes it more attractive, not less so. Overdose means, after all, a better product.

The color and consistency of the heroin available in the street varies, too. It ranges from a white or brownish powder to the black sticky substance sold mainly on the West Coast and known as Mexican black tar. Mexico is one of the three traditional regions where heroin is produced. The other two are the "golden triangle" in Southeast Asia (Laos, Thailand, Burma) and the "golden crescent" of the Pakistan-Afghanistan-Iran area. Recently, Central and South America have also joined the market.

ORIGIN AND CHEMISTRY

Heroin belongs to the opiate family, a group of drugs extracted from opium—the milky juice from the unripe seed capsules of the poppy plant *Papaver somniferum*. Heroin is not actually extracted from opium, but morphine is. Heroin is synthesized (produced) by introducing two acetyl groups (organic molecules derived from the metabolism of carbohydrates or fats) into the morphine molecule. So, strictly speaking, heroin is an opioid—the group of synthetic drugs that have pharmacological properties similar to opium and morphine. In a generic sense, though, the terms are considered interchangeable.

Opiates are known for their powerful ability to relieve pain (analgesia), promote euphoria (feeling of well-being), and sedation (relaxed state). Although morphine was introduced only 200 years ago, and heroin 100 years later, opiates in their crude form, opium, have been used by humans for over 6,000 years. References to opium appear in inscriptions and texts of ancient Sumer, Egypt, and

Greece. The Romans ate it baked in cakes, and it is still eaten in India, Turkey, Afghanistan, and other countries where the opium poppy is cultivated. Fifty percent of the opium eaters in India take it as a pill or as a solution for medicinal purposes.

As a medicine, opium was introduced in the thirteenth century by Arab traders in India. By the seventeenth century, the Chinese had devised a method of smoking it by using long pipes. In the nineteenth century, opium was a very important item of trade for the British in India. They exported the drug to China, where a large percentage of the population became addicted to it.

Opium came to America on the *Mayflower* in 1620. It was brought by the Puritans from England mixed with wine and spices in bottles labeled laudanum, or mixed with licorice, honey, benzoic acid, camphor, and anise oil as a tincture called paregoric. Since its early introduction to America, it has remained, for better or for worse, a part of American life.

During the eighteenth century, many scientists in Europe tried to isolate the active agent in opium. In 1806, Friedrich Sertuerner of Hanover, Germany, a 20-year-old pharmacist's helper, was the first to isolate opium's active agent, morphine. Sertuerner took the name "morphine" from Morpheus, the Greek god of dreams, because of morphine's sedating properties. It was the first drug compound ever to be isolated from a plant.

Morphine would prove ten times more potent than opium as a painkiller. The invention of the hypodermic syringe in the 1840s allowed the drug to be introduced directly into the bloodstream. Injected this way, morphine provided even stronger and faster effects on the user. Morphine is also habit-forming and has the same toxic effects as opium.

These problems became apparent when many soldiers

treated with morphine during the Civil War became addicted. As the use of morphine as a household medicine continued to spread, so too did addiction.

Heroin (3,6-diacetyl-morphine) was first synthesized in 1874 by the British chemist C.R.A. Wright. When one of his colleagues tested the new drug on dogs, the results were so discouraging that the drug was abandoned.

Two decades later, it was the German scientist Heinrich Dreser working for the Bayer Company—then the most powerful chemical company in the world—who had the inspiration to test the drug for human respiratory disease. His was not a broad investigation of the drug effects, but a clear example of a scientist setting his experiments to get the answer he is looking for. If morphine had worked in the past in relieving cough, then diacetyl-morphine should work too, Dreser probably reasoned. When Dreser started his tests on the Bayer employees, he narrowed his search to see the effects of the drug on the lungs and minimized the importance of any unwanted results.

The introduction of two esters (compounds formed by the reaction of the alcohol group with an acid) onto the morphine molecule increases its solubility, allowing the preparation of solutions with a higher drug concentration. Heroin is also more potent than morphine. One gram of heroin produces the effects of 2 to 4 grams of morphine. From a commercial point of view, the conversion of morphine into heroin increases both the potency and the value of the drug.

In 1898 when the Bayer businessmen proudly introduced the new drug, they called it heroin because they believed it to be the "heroic" cure against the most lethal disease in the industrialized world, the Great White Plague of the time—tuberculosis.

In an unfortunate turn of events in the late twentieth century, heroin actually resurrected tuberculosis as an epidemiological problem at a time when the disease had been

This is the molecular structure of heroin, $C_{21}H_{23}NO_5$. Heroin was first synthesized by British chemist C.R.A. Wright in 1874. After brief studies of the drug's effect in animal testing, Wright and his colleagues concluded that heroin offered no significant medical benefits and abandoned their research.

almost totally eradicated. This was the same disease that 100 years earlier heroin was believed to cure.

For 16 years after its introduction, heroin was widely and easily available in drug and grocery stores and by mail order as a sedative for coughs. Later, when its painkilling properties became evident, it was widely accepted in the medical community as a "cure" for opium and morphine dependence. Not surprisingly, by the 1920s, heroin had become the most widely abused of the opiates. When it was finally declared illegal in 1924, however, heroin's formula was so well known that many illegal prduction operations quickly sprung up to satisfy the public's craving for the drug.

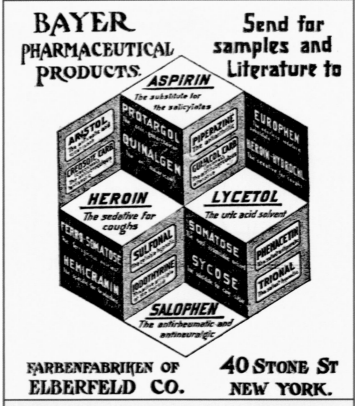

The tuberculosis epidemic in the late nineteenth century prompted the German-based Bayer Company to claim that heroin could cure many respiratory diseases without the toxic and addictive effects of codeine or morphine. This advertisement for Bayer aspirin shows heroin as one of Bayer's main products.

WAYS OF INTAKE

Heroin is not the easiest drug to introduce into the body. First, it makes more first-time users sick than with other drugs. Then, there is the needle. In many states, it is illegal to sell hypodermic needles without a prescription, which forces users to buy them on the street or share them with other users, thereby increasing the risk of infection from a contaminated needle.

In the past, most people, mainly young people who have grown up under the threat of AIDS, would dismiss the idea of injecting themselves and move away from heroin. This is no longer the case, however. The heroin found in the streets now is so pure—up to 94 percent pure in some cases—that it works even when snorted or smoked. In fact, according to a National Institute of Drug Abuse (NIDA) December 1999 survey, the route of administration among heroin users admitted for treatment in several major U.S. cities has shifted dramatically from injecting to snorting and smoking. In some cities, such as New York, Newark, and Chicago, sniffing or snorting is the most common means of taking heroin.

Although heroin is still addictive and its side effects are the same whatever the route of intake, 40 percent of high school seniors polled by NIDA in 1999 did not believe there was any risk in trying heroin. Thus, even without the risks and social stigma associated with using a needle, heroin had lured many young people under 18 into its grasp.

"Chasing the dragon," (a slang term for smoking heroin) is sometimes done by dusting a tobacco cigarette with heroin. More frequently, however, it involves putting the drug on a piece of tin foil and heating it with a match. The heroin blackens and wriggles like a snake—or dragon's tail—as it burns and produces fumes that are inhaled through a straw.

Taken either through the nose by snorting or by smoking, the heroin molecules eventually reach the lungs. After entering the bloodstream through the capillaries that surround the alveoli (small sacs along the walls of the lungs), the molecules arrive at the central nervous system. Once the heroin molecules reach the central nervous system (a few minutes after intake), users feel an overwhelming sense of well-being rushing through their bodies—a warm feeling that begins in the lower spinal area and runs through the central nervous system. This overwhelming feeling is what addicts refer to simply as "the rush." This feeling is so powerful that after a

Madison and Jessica could hear the music pounding as they walked up the driveway to Steve's party. Of course, Madison wasn't surprised when Jessica ditched her to go flirt with her "flavor of the week."

"Do you want to dance?"

She didn't have to look up to know it was Steve. Just as she was about to brush him off, Matt appeared in the doorway. Madison wondered why he looked so happy after just dumping her a few hours earlier, but then Mona walked in and gave Matt a little squeeze around the waist. (Madison couldn't stand Mona with her blond hair and big fake smile.)

"So, have you made up your mind or what?" Steve asked.

Normally, she would never dance with Steve, but today wasn't a normal day.

"Sure, why not?" she said, and grabbed Steve's hand.

The party was winding down and Jessica had already taken off when Steve led Madison into one of the back rooms in the house. Two guys she barely knew were sitting on the floor by a coffee table—one of them was heating a spoon with a match, while the other was laying back against the sofa. There was a syringe on the table and a belt or something coiled by it. Madison turned to leave.

Steve grabbed her hand. "Come on, Madison. It's only smack."

"I don't like needles."

"Afraid of AIDS?" he laughs. "We're all clean here."

She shook her head.

"OK, OK. You don't have to shoot. Snort some. No harm done that way. Come on. I'll show you how."

Steve produced a bag and spilled some powder on the table, forming a line. Fascinated, Madison watched him snort the neat line of powdered heroin with a rolled-up ten dollar bill.

What Madison doesn't know is that although she may have been avoiding potential exposure to HIV/AIDS by not injecting heroin, there is no such thing as "just smack." Nausea and vomiting often accompany the rush a first-time user feels. If a first-time user takes too much heroin, or heroin that is too pure, he or she may experience an overdose that results in death.

person has experienced it once, he or she will often do anything to experience it again. Achieving this same rush, or sense of euphoria, however, may not be so easy. Because of the property of "tolerance" inherent in the very nature of this harmless-looking substance, the user will need increasingly higher doses of the drug and/or a more effective way of introducing it into the body to produce the same effect.

PROGRESS TO INJECTION

Heroin can be injected intramuscularly (into a muscle) or subcutaneously (under the skin) in what is called "skin popping." By far the most common way of taking heroin is "mainlining" or "shooting"—that is, direct injection of the drug into the vein. Addicts perform the "ritual" that precedes the shot with an almost religious zeal. (This ritual is such an important part of the experience that when admitted into a rehabilitation program, some addicts have reported missing the ritual almost as much as the rush itself.)

The ritual involves pouring heroin from the glassine envelope into a metal spoon, heating the spoon to dissolve the powdered heroin into a liquid, and injecting this liquid heroin into a vein.

SHORT-TERM EFFECTS

Within 30 to 60 seconds of injection, heroin produces a surge of pleasurable emotions (the rush) that lasts for about one minute. This is followed by a warm flushing of the skin, a contraction of the pupils (miosis), dry mouth, a heavy feeling in the arms and legs, and feeling of sleepiness (the nod). Stress, anxiety, and physical pain are reduced.

Unwanted effects that usually accompany heroin intake are nausea, vomiting, severe itching, and, sometimes, spontaneous abortion in pregnant women. A strong dose of heroin also results in constipation (due to an increased tone of the sphincter and a decreased propulsive movement of the intestines) and difficulty in urination (due to an increased tone of the bladder sphincter and urethra).

After the injection, the user is drowsy for several hours. Mental function is clouded by the heroin's effect on the central nervous system, the cardiac function slows, and breathing is depressed, sometimes so severely that it even stops.

The pharmacological effects of heroin are identical with those of morphine. This probably reflects the fact that heroin has a very short half-life in the blood. (Half-life is the amount of time it takes the body to eliminate half of the drug molecules from the bloodstream.) As soon as heroin enters the bloodstream, it is hydrolyzed (split by the addition of liquid) by esterases (enzymes that break certain kinds of chemical bonds called ester bonds). The acetyl group at the 3-position is far more sensitive to these enzymes than the acetyl group at the 6-position. In fact, the 3-acetyl group is attacked almost immediately after injection, and, within several minutes, virtually all the heroin is converted to a metabolite, 6-acetlymorphine. The remaining acetyl group at the 6-position is also lost, but at a slower rate. Loss of both acetyl groups in the body generates morphine. It is believed that a combination of 6-acetylmorphine and morphine is responsible for the effects of heroin.

BRAIN RECEPTORS AND NATURAL OPIATES

Opiate molecules produce their effects on the human body by binding to receptors on specific neurons of the central nervous system. The central nervous system (the brain and spinal cord) controls all functions in the body. It is a complex structure that has two main types of cells: structural support cells, or glia, and neurons, which are cells that receive and transmit information. The main areas of the brain that are affected by opiate drugs are the cerebral cortex, the limbic system, the thalamus, the hypothalamus, and the brain stem.

The cerebral cortex, (or more simply, the cortex) is the highest functional area of the brain. It is responsible for memory storage and sensory, integrative, emotional, language, and motor functions, i.e., nearly all of the complex sensory and perceptual tasks that are required to function effectively.

The limbic system is a group of structures within the brain that are associated with various emotions and feelings such as anger, fear, sexual arousal, pleasure, and sadness. It is from here that the brain's reward system eminates.

The thalamus is a sensory structure in the brain that serves as a relay center for impulses to and from the cerebral cortex. Located below the cortex, the thalamus also registers sensations such as pain, temperature, and touch.

The hypothalamus activates, controls, and integrates the peripheral autonomic nervous system (the part of the nervous system that regulates involuntary vital functions such as cardiac muscle, smooth muscle, and glands), endocrine processes, and many somatic functions such as body temperature, sleep, and appetite. Located on top of the brain stem, the hypothalamus controls such vital feelings as hunger and thirst.

The brain stem is the portion of the brain that contains, among other things, the vital centers—the respiratory, vasomotor, and cardiac centers. These are called vital because they are necessary for survival. Other essential functions that originate here are vomiting, hiccupping, sneezing, coughing, and swallowing reflexes.

Four types of opioid receptors have been identified in the central nervous system: mu (μ), kappa (κ), delta (δ), and sigma (σ). Heroin (morphine) effects are mediated mainly by its interaction with mu and kappa receptors. Both receptors are involved with analgesia. Mu receptors are especially abundant in the limbic system, thalamus, hypothalamus, and brain stem; kappa receptors are abundant in the cerebral cortex and spinal cord.

Mu receptors mediate the euphoric effects of opiates in the reward circuit (situated in the hypothalamus). They also mediate analgesia, as well as respiratory depression; some of the constipation associated with narcotic use; excessive sweating; nausea (with initial vomiting which is later suppressed); and cough suppression. Kappa receptors mediate analgesia at the spinal-cord level, miosis (contraction of the pupils), and much of the sedation, as well as some of the constipation.

Why would the central nervous system have evolved in such a way to include receptors that bind opiate molecules? Why should a human cell go through the trouble of synthesizing these complex proteins and target them to the neuron membranes to sit there and wait for the improbable appearance in the bloodstream of an alkaloid from the sap of a poppy plant? The logical explanation is that the human body has its own natural opioids.

In 1975, at the University of Aberdeen in Scotland, John Hughes and Hans Kosterlitz isolated two peptides with a high affinity for opioid receptors. They called them enkephalins (meaning "in the head"). Almost simultaneously in Baltimore, Maryland, Solomon Snyder, Gavril Pasternak, and Rabi Simantov found similar compounds in the human brain.

Neuropeptides and Their Mimickers

Although the similarity between morphine and neuropeptides (peptides that affect the neurons) is merely structural (morphine is an alkaloid not a peptide), it is this structural similarity that allows the morphine molecule to fit into the receptor site, in much the same way as a key fits into a lock. Once the receptor is activated, the morphine elicits the same response that natural neuropeptides would. Because the reaction is out of context and amplified, owing to the higher concentration of opiates, the result is a biochemical imbalance that the body was not designed for—in other words, disease.

To date, three types of neuroactive peptides have been identified: enkephalins, endorphins, and dynorphins. Although they vary in size, they all share a tetra peptide sequence Tyr-Gly-Gly-Phe. This sequence is essential to their

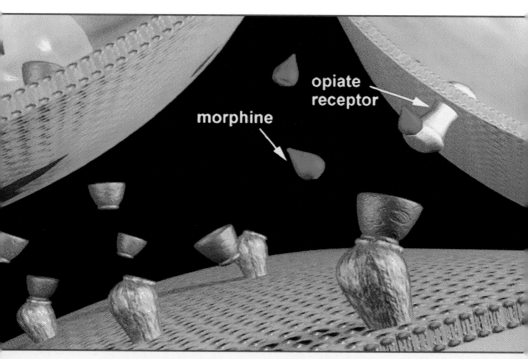

This representation of a synapse between two neurons in the brain shows the action of opiates at opiate receptors. Enzymes in the brain convert heroin to morphine. When morphine binds to opiate receptors (yellow), it mimics the action of naturally-occurring chemicals in the brain called endorphins. The binding of morphine (green) to the receptor at the right (yellow) sends a signal to the neuron on the left to release increased amounts of a neurotransmitter called dopamine (blue), a key neurotransmitter in the brain's reward system. It is the increased levels of dopamine created by heroin that produce the pleasure a heroin user feels.

function. If any of these amino acids are removed or modified, the peptide loses its activity.

Enkephalins behave as inhibitory neurotransmitters (i.e., molecules released by neurons to stimulate or inhibit the activity of the neuron). They bind to opiate receptors in the dorsal horn of the spinal cord and block the release of substance P. Substance P is a transmitter of pain impulses in the nerve fibers. By blocking its release, the enkephalins decrease the perception and emotional aspect of pain. Because enkephalins were first discovered for their ability to bind to the same neuroreceptors that morphine did, they were called internal opiates or natural painkillers.

Endorphins is a general term that includes many peptides found not only in the brain but also in the pituitary gland, the intermediate lobe, and the corticotrophin cells of the adenohypophysis (front part of the pituitary gland). Several subgroups of endorphins have been isolated and identified, including b-endorphin, an analgesic substance that is much more potent than enkephalin.

Enkephalins and B-endorphins are both found in the brain, pituitary gland, and gastrointestinal tract but not in the same cells.

Dynorphin is an endorphin found in the pituitary gland, hypothalamus, and spinal cord. It is the most potent pain-relieving substance ever discovered; dynorphin is 50 times more potent than b-endorphin and 200 times more potent than morphine.

The body produces natural opioids to relieve pain and prevent shock in moments of stress. During childbirth, endorphins are released at a rate up to ten times the normal level, likely as a protective mechanism to ease the stress and pain for the mother and child. Endorphins are also said to be responsible for the "high" that some athletes claim to experience after running a long distance. Again, this may be the body's way of coping with stress and pain. Endorphin release in the body is also higher after acupuncture and transcutaneous electrical nerve stimulation, which may explain their therapeutic results.

When a person takes heroin, the normal production of neuropeptides in the brain decreases. If the heroin administration ceases, the body goes through a period of adjustment until the production of its own neuropeptides returns to normal levels. This adjustment period is called withdrawal.

Most of the effects of opiates are caused by their ability to mimic neuropeptides, the natural opiates of the brain, and to interact with their receptors mainly in three specific regions of the central nervous system: the limbic system, the brain stem, and the spinal cord. Since the limbic system controls emotion, heroin increases the feeling of pleasure. Since the brain stem controls the automatic functions of the body, heroin is reported to depress breathing. Heroin also blocks pain messages from the spinal cord to the brain which explains its pain relief properties.

2

Long-Term Effects of Heroin

The two most feared effects of heroin use are addiction and death by overdose. Death by overdose is the result of taking too much heroin. Addiction, on the other hand, is an elusive concept whose meaning seems to shift shape and adapt to each person's perception.

Some view addiction as a spiritual weakness, a way of life chosen by those who don't want to take responsibility for their actions. For others, addiction is a normal, natural consequence of the way the brain is wired. Some claim addiction is a disease. Others believe it is a complex behavior driven by chemical processes in the brain. Some prefer the term "addictive behaviors" to "addiction," whereas the World Health Organization suggests calling it "drug dependence" and differentiates between physical and psychological dependence.

Although it is clear to some that heroin causes addiction, not all experts agree. Heroin is not the problem, they say. Blaming heroin for addiction is like blaming the car for causing an accident. Addiction is created by the person, not the drug.

REINFORCEMENT AND THE BRAIN REWARD SYSTEM

To address reinforcement and reward, let us start from the beginning. Before addiction exists, there is just a substance—heroin—and a potential user. Addiction can happen only if the user takes the heroin and if the experience it gives the person is so pleasurable that he or she wants to try it again.

Heroin (morphine 6-acetylmorphine) molecules exert their powerful effects by working directly on the limbic, or reward system

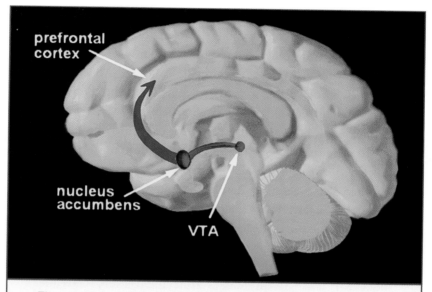

prefrontal cortex

nucleus accumbens

VTA

The reward system in the brain originates in a group of neurons in the midbrain called the ventral tegmental area (VTA). When heroin molecules bind to receptors within these neurons of the VTA, the neurons release the neurotransmitter dopamine into the cortex and the nucleus accumbens of the basil ganglia. It is this release of dopamine into the nucleus accumbens that produces the overall feeling of pleasure in the heroin user. Albeit through differing mechanisms, all addictive drugs somehow increase the dopamine levels in the nucleus accumbens.

of the brain. When functioning normally, the limbic system's job is to create commands that tell the body to seek food, water, and the like. But heroin changes the way the limbic system works. Instead of commands that tell our bodies to seek food, water, and sustenance, heroin causes the limbic system to create commands that tell the body to seek more heroin. Why does heroin have this effect on the brain?

Heroin achieves its effects by binding to opiate receptors within the neurons of the ventral tegmental area (VTA) of the brain reward system. (In fact, the one thing all addictive drugs have in common is that they turn on the brain reward system.) Without the introduction of heroin into the body, dopamine release is kept in check by a neurotransmitter, GABA (gamma-aminobutyric acid), that inhibits the release of dopamine. Once heroin is introduced into the body and finds its way to the brain, it binds to the opiate receptors contained in GABA, thereby interfering with GABA's normal dopamine-inhibiting effects. It is the release of dopamine that is ultimately responsible for the intense feeling of pleasure that the heroin user experiences.

It is a simple case of psychological conditioning, in which a behavior (injecting heroin) precedes a reinforcement (feeling soothed). Because street heroin is adulterated and its purity is unreliable, the reinforcement (reward) does not occur every time, and the user will have to keep using it in the hope of getting the reward. This behavior persists even when followed by undesirable consequences such as violence or arrest by the police. In fact, intermittent reinforcement strengthens the psychological conditioning. A heroin addict keeps injecting in search of a high, just as the gambler continues playing in spite of losses.

The brain's reward circuit appeared early in evolution. In every animal from fish to humans, this circuit in the brain is ready to be turned on when the opiate receptors are activated. When the opiate receptors are activated, the animal experiences an immediate gratification which provides a reason for doing certain activities necessary for survival. Survival can mean survival of the individual, as in eating and drinking, or survival of the species, as in having sex and nurturing the young. In other words, activation of opiate receptors reinforces these activities. Reinforcement is chronologically the first characteristic of addiction.

Of course, the reward circuit did not evolve to react to morphine molecules. But the reward system is there, and heroin uses it. There is nothing abnormal about getting high on heroin. There is a natural basis for this, which means that the capacity for addiction is in all of us. It is what the users bring to the experience that determines whether or not they become addicted.

TOLERANCE

Continued use of heroin induces tolerance. In the case of drug use and addiction, tolerance refers to the need to take higher doses of the drug to produce the same effects. A tolerant user may require 50 to 100 times the initial dose to provide a brief high. But tolerance has a limit. The user doesn't have to increase the dose indefinitely; eventually the user reaches a plateau at which he or she will feel satisfied.

Tolerance to opiates may or may not develop when opiates are used to treat pain in a medical setting. Some patients with cancer find that the same dose of morphine is enough to stop their pain over a period of months. Others can develop remarkable tolerance and need up to 1000 milligrams of morphine per hour—the starting therapeutic dose is 10 to 15 milligrams by injection every four to six hours. However, doses of more than 60 milligrams can cause fatal respiratory depressions in nontolerant individuals.

Because not all opiate users develop tolerance, some people, for example, Richard L. Miller, believe that tolerance to heroin is a psychological and not a pharmacological phenomenon. He believes that tolerance springs not from the drug, but from the reason that the user takes it.

PHYSICAL DEPENDENCE

If a person takes heroin regularly, his or her body adapts to the presence of the drug and needs the drug to function normally. Although this effect is usually called physical dependence, the term is not totally accurate. A heroin addict is not physically dependent on heroin the way a diabetic is dependent on insulin. Without insulin, the diabetic will die. Without heroin, a user will get sick, but eventually will adapt and feel better. To reach physical dependence, the user must overcome the negative effects of heroin, such as nausea and a queasy stomach, which accompany an intoxicating dose of heroin.

In 1964, a classic study of New York City heroin users concluded that physical dependence does not develop if a person takes heroin less than once a day. In a 1983 study of pure heroin use, the subjects needed to take the drug three times a day for two weeks to develop a physical dependence. In medical settings, it has been shown that some people can take morphine injections one or two times a day for years without appreciable dependence.

WITHDRAWAL

When regular heroin users stop taking the drug, they experience withdrawal symptoms. These symptoms usually appear within 12 hours after the last dose of heroin and can last as long as 72 to 96 hours, with a peak at about 36 to 48 hours. The severity of the symptoms is related to the amount of the dose and the frequency of abuse. A person who uses a low dose or does not use heroin regularly will have symptoms similar to the

THE FACE OF ADDICTION

In 1950, Chet Baker, the golden boy of California jazz, had everything—talent, looks, and the adoration of both men and women. By the time of his taped appearance on a television documentary in 1988—his once angel-looking face looking more like a death mask as he extolled the virtues of heroin-and-cocaine speedballs—he had been dead for months. Whether he was pushed by an angry dealer or jumped in a drug-induced stupor, Baker's life had been claimed by heroin long before his head hit a concrete post three floors below his hotel room window in Amsterdam, Netherlands.

Sid Vicious was the charismatic bassist of the Sex Pistols when he met Nancy Spungeon, a heroin-addicted groupie from Pennsylvania, who introduced him to the drug. Obsessed with each other and their next high, the couple retreated farther and farther from the world. After weeks of sitting in a room at the Chelsea Hotel in New York City, shooting up day and night, Spungeon died from a wound that Vicious accidentally inflicted on her. Several months later, at age 21, Sid Vicious overdosed.

flu that last a day or two. For a heavier user, the symptoms will last longer.

Typical withdrawal symptoms include sneezing, runny nose, hot and cold flashes, nausea, stomach cramps and vomiting, diarrhea, and gooseflesh (this is why sudden withdrawal is popularly called "going cold turkey"); hyperventilation, hypothermia, mydriasis (excessive dilation of the pupils), and inability to focus the eyes; joint pain, tremors, and twitching movements, particularly of the feet (that is why withdrawal is also called "kicking the habit"); and elevated pulse rate, blood pressure, and temperature.

Once the initial stage of withdrawal is past, usually within five days, a secondary phase of protracted symptoms may last several months. These symptoms include low blood pressure, dilated pupils, and a general listlessness.

Although very uncomfortable, withdrawal symptoms are not life-threatening, except to the fetus of an addicted mother. This is why sudden withdrawal of heroin in pregnant women is not recommended.

Although the complete biological mechanism of withdrawal symptoms is not fully understood, some of these symptoms can be explained as a rebound effect. For example, heroin provokes constipation; in fact, it was once used to treat loose bowels. During use, the body adjusts in an effort to keep bowel movements normal. If heroin supply stops, compensating efforts continue until the body chemistry rebounds to normal and a temporary diarrhea may result.

At a biochemical level, the withdrawal symptoms reflect stimulation of previously depressed neurons.

ADDICTION

Physical dependence and the emergence of withdrawal symptoms were once believed the only characteristics necessary for addiction. A person who had physical dependence was called an addict. A person without dependence was not an addict. Experience has shown that these statements are not accurate.

Although dependence and withdrawal symptoms are a part of addiction, they are not the whole picture.

The key signs of addiction are morbid craving and a mental focus on obtaining and using the heroin. The entire life of an addict revolves around obtaining the drug. Equating addiction with physical dependence simplifies the diagnosis. Physical dependence can be measured by its withdrawal symptoms, whereas craving cannot be measured. Having symptoms of withdrawal does not make a user an addict. For instance, in a medical setting, patients who use opioids to treat chronic pain usually do not have problems leaving the drug after their pain is gone. If a person does not want to take the drug, he or she is not addicted.

On the other hand, a person without symptoms of withdrawal is an addict if he or she still has the craving. Part of the craving may be physical, as in wanting to stop the discomfort of the withdrawal symptoms, but the symptoms are not severe enough to justify the aggravation and debasement that the addict must go through to maintain the addiction.

In many cases, the craving reappears months or years after withdrawal symptoms are gone. For instance, if heroin was used to meet a certain need, such as to assuage feelings of inadequacy or guilt, when that need returns, the person will look for the drug to fill the need, even after the withdrawal symptoms are gone. The craving can also be triggered by returning to the places where the addict formerly took heroin or by being with the friends he or she associates with the addiction.

Because symptoms of withdrawal and craving seem to be unrelated, some people claim there is no pharmacological basis for addiction, and that it is the morbid craving that leads to addiction, not the addiction to the craving. Along these lines of thinking, psychologists like Stanton Peele claim that drugs are not physically addictive, but merely a way the user achieves feelings and rewards he does not feel he can achieve any other way. The drug that the addict chooses may have a

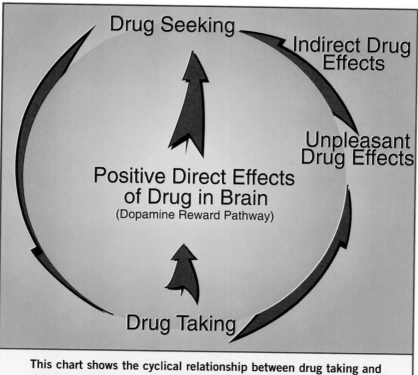

This chart shows the cyclical relationship between drug taking and drug seeking; taking a drug like heroin stimulates the reward pathway in the brain, which urges the user to seek more of the drug, which leads to drug taking again. Indirect drug effects, like a particular setting or memory associated with taking the drug, can also lead to drug seeking.

basis in chemistry and in the effects the drug has on the body. For instance, a person troubled by anxiety, anger, or frustration may crave the calming relief of narcotic intoxication. However, addiction is symptomatic of a something missing in the user's life, not the drug.

Even those who believe drug addiction involves physical dependence, tolerance, and morbid craving agree that these factors alone do not make an addict. The crucial factor in addiction is the frame of mind that the person brings to the experience, his or her reasons for taking heroin.

3

The Health Effects of Heroin

The human body is a complex interaction of chemicals. Any foreign substance—prescribed or illegal—added to this mixture challenges its balance and disrupts its normal functioning. In the case of a prescription drug, the change is wanted—at least the specific change the drug is taken to affect. Once the drug enters the body, though, it is bound to affect not only the targeted organ, but also any organ susceptible to its particular molecular structure.

From a medical perspective, the desirable effects of a prescription drug are praised and used in marketing advertisements. The undesirable effects are called side effects and written in small letters on the prescription label. Heroin was once a prescription drug. First, it was marketed as a cure for tuberculosis and other respiratory illnesses; later as an analgesic. Respiratory depression and analgesia are indeed two of the effects heroin has on the human body. They are not the only ones. By binding to the opioid receptors, the heroin metabolites (substances yielded by metabolism of heroin) mimic all the effects that endorphins have on the body. With heroin intake, the effect is amplified and out of context. For instance, endorphins are implicated in feelings of sedation and happiness. There is nothing wrong with being happy, except when the behavior does not fit the circumstances.

Most opioid receptors are located in the brain, spinal cord, and in the membrane of the intestines. Heroin inhibits the bowel movements by binding directly to these last receptors. It depresses

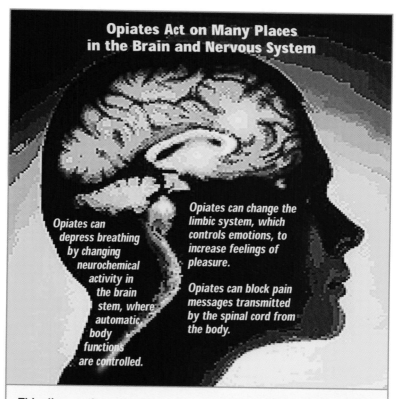

Opiates Act on Many Places in the Brain and Nervous System

Opiates can depress breathing by changing neurochemical activity in the brain stem, where automatic body functions are controlled.

Opiates can change the limbic system, which controls emotions, to increase feelings of pleasure.

Opiates can block pain messages transmitted by the spinal cord from the body.

This diagram from the National Institute on Drug Abuse highlights some of the health effects experienced in the brain and nervous system during opiate use. The human body is a complex and delicate system which will be influenced by the introduction of any foreign substance.

breathing and dulls the pain signals coming from the body by binding to receptors in certain groups of neurons, and it reduces sexual activity by altering the activity of the neurons that regulate secretion of hormones.

Hormones are natural chemical substances secreted into the bloodstream from the endocrine glands. The reproductive organs or gonads produce ova or sperm and also secrete hormones (sexual hormones) that initiate and maintain the secondary sexual characteristics in men and women. The sexual hormones themselves are regulated by other hormones secreted by the pituitary gland (a pea-sized gland situated in the brain).

After heroin ingestion, the production of the female hormone prolactin increases, and release of luteinizing hormone decreases. Prolactin is the hormone associated with lactation; the luteinizing hormone affects ovary function and sperm production. In the female, menstrual cycles may cease or be altered. Although female infertility is also common, women can get pregnant. If they do, they will have a higher risk of miscarriage or of giving birth to twins or triplets or babies with birth defects. Repeated use of heroin during pregnancy leads to the baby being born physically addicted to the drug. These babies are restless and irritable. In extreme cases, they may suffer convulsions or die. Heroin affects male hormones as well. As a result of hormonal changes from heroin, male sperm production decreases, resulting in infertility.

Heroin abuse causes mental problems. Of these, addiction is the most severe, and depression is the most common. Depression afflicts one in six heroin abusers and one in three of those who are trying to give up the drug. Heroin can also cause frightening hallucinations.

The effects of heroin in adolescents are even more dramatic. In a growing body, the cells divide faster and the drug moves faster into and through the body systems. Also, because the immune system is not completely developed, fighting the foreign substance puts a greater strain on the system.

Sexual development, beginning in humans at about age 11 and continuing for several years, can be delayed or stunted by heroin abuse. Both the general growth and the sexual development must take place during adolescence. If it doesn't, the person will never reach his or her growing potential.

Heroin affects mental development, too. Intellectual learning, the learning of moral and ethical values, and the development of the emotions and the ways to express them occur from birth to the early 20s. If the adolescent uses drugs during these years, he or she may never learn the skills necessary to survive and succeed in the world.

Heroin use also affects the health, sexuality, emotional ties, and intellectual functioning of adults. When adults stop using the drug, they have an adult self to return to, the self they were before. An adolescent who started using drugs at a young age will return to the same patterns of behavior of the boy or girl who started taking the drug.

OVERDOSE

Apart from disrupting the body and mind, heroin kills. The overall death rate among heroin addicts is 16 times higher than the death rate among people of the same age group who do not use heroin. This is especially tragic if we consider that heroin addicts are usually between the ages of 15 and 30, a time when the death rate is normally very low. Needless to say, 87 percent of all deaths among heroin addicts result from an overdose.

Overdose or heroin toxicity is a consequence of ingesting too much heroin. When this happens, the user's skin turns cold, clammy-looking, and eventually blue. The user becomes stuporous and may have seizures. If the amount is large enough, he or she may die.

Overdose occurs because heroin disrupts the signals that the neurons on the brain stem, which controls breathing, send to the diaphragm and lungs. As a consequence, breathing slows down to as few as two to four breaths per minute. This causes the blood pressure and body temperature to drop. Quick intervention by injection of an opiate antagonist, such as naltrexone or naloxone, can reverse these effects. If untreated, the person who has overdosed will slip into a coma, and within 20 to 30 minutes respiratory failure and death follow.

Opiate antagonists are molecules that bind to the same receptors that opiates do, but they do not produce any effects. They are the wrong key to open the door, but they still block

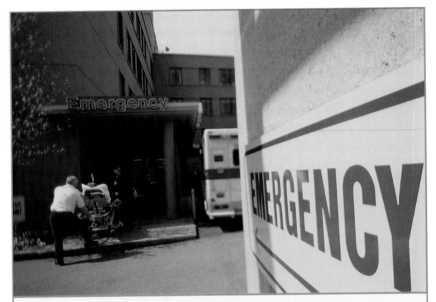

Heroin overdoses often occur when a user miscalculates the amount of a dose or the purity of a particular batch of the drug. According to statistics from the Drug Abuse Warning Network, there were 96,000 heroin-related emergency department admissions in the United States in 2000.

other keys from accessing the keyhole. Antagonists stop the effects of the morphine molecules by displacing them from the opioid receptors. The result is an immediate state of withdrawal that restores the victim's breathing. The first breaths a person takes after an overdose are painful. As the air comes into the lungs, the victim feels a burning sensation. To ease this symptom, oxygen is administered.

Most often a heroin overdose is due to the unknown purity of street heroin that is taken. This is what killed two friends in June 1994 in Florida when they had their first experience with heroin. At about the same time, pure heroin started pouring into the United States and probably is what killed River Phoenix, a talented 21-year-old actor, who appeared in movies such as *Stand by Me* and *Running on Empty*, outside a bar.

Overdose can also occur by miscalculation. After going through a detoxification program, the addict's tolerance to the drug diminishes. If the person has a relapse and takes the dose that he or she was used to before detoxification, the result will probably be an overdose.

Some people overdose on purpose, thinking suicide is the only way out of an unmanageable life.

ADDICTION AS A DISEASE

The concept of addiction being a disease rather than some aberrant behavioral problem began to advance in the years following Prohibition. During the Prohibition era of the 1920s and 1930s, alcohol was "evil" and no one could use it safely. When it became evident that the social and economic costs of outlawing alcohol were intolerably high and that Prohibition had to stop, legislators needed a new model that would allow them to make drinking permissible again and save face at the same time. That is how the idea of addiction as a disease started. There are two groups of people, as the proposition goes: one has the disease and the other does not. The first group cannot handle alcohol. The rest of the population can. Soon this model was also extended to drug abuse.

Today, the concept of addiction as a disease is widespread. According to the U.S. Department of Health and Human Services, addiction is a "common, potentially life threatening, chronic disease that affects approximately ten percent of American adults and three percent of adolescents."

Taking the metaphor of addiction as a disease a step farther, the media has sometimes called heroin use a "drug epidemic." This metaphor, apart from causing unjustified panic in the population, is incorrect. Although the spread of heroin use does follow the mathematical models of an epidemic, unlike catching an infectious disease, drug use is a voluntary act. Drugs do not strike at random like bacteria and viruses. The only person at risk is the one who decides to use the drug. Heroin use is a dangerous fad, transmitted through word of mouth from friend to friend, not an infectious disease.

Some experts do not agree with the general theory on addiction. They think that labeling addiction as a disease is too simplistic and does not cover all the aspects and complexity of addiction. Disease or not, taking heroin affects the user's health. Apart from the risk of addiction or death by overdose, heroin addicts usually eat poorly because they prefer to spend their money on the drug. This leads to malnourishment and vitamin deficiencies that make them susceptible to infections.

OTHER MEDICAL COMPLICATIONS

Apart from the medical complications caused directly by the chemical properties of heroin, its primary method of intake—injection—is the source of further health problems.

Some problems are directly skin related. Most are caused by the transmittal of disease through the use of unsterile needles and the sharing of such needles. Unfortunately, washing needles in a public toilet is a common practice. While the hypodermic needle is the primary means of drug injection, drug addicts who do not have access to hypodermics use such dangerous substitutes as lancets or scalpels, or any small sharp blade to make an opening. Then they insert an eyedropper, tubing, and bulb and squirt the drug into the wound. The risk of serious infection with this method is high.

However, the use of a needle is not that much safer. The veins in the arms, the ones usually first injected, collapse easily. So other veins—on the feet, neck, leg, and other places—must be used. Chet Baker, the 1950s jazz trumpeter and singer, boasted to a friend that he had over 3,000 punctures on his arms.

Heroin addicts frequently have cellulitis (inflammation of deep tissues), skin abscesses (deep sores in the skin), and ulcerated areas (called "burns" in street vernacular) from injecting heroin under the skin (skin-popping). Abscesses can become infected with the tetanus bacteria. Tetanus causes muscle

Short- and Long-Term Effects of Heroin Abuse

Short-Term Effects	Long-Term Effects
"Rush"	Addiction
Depressed respiration	Infectious diseases, for example, HIV/AIDS and hepatitis B and C
Clouded mental functioning	Collapsed veins
Nausea and vomiting	Bacterial infections
Suppression of pain	Abscesses
Spontaneous abortion	Infection of heart lining and valves
	Arthritis and other rheumatologic problems

This table from the National Household Survey on Drug Abuse (NHSDA) lists the short- and long-term effects of heroin abuse. To compile the descriptions of these health effects, the NHSDA surveyed people in all 50 states and asked them questions about their drug use and related experiences.

spasms, usually in the jaws and muscles of the neck. That is why it is called "lockjaw." Tetanus often causes death in addicts. Among female addicts, the death rate from tetanus is as high as 90 percent.

Injecting heroin may cause blood clots. If a blood clot reaches a vital organ such as the heart or brain, it causes sudden death. If clots block the lungs, embolic pneumonia develops. Pneumonia is an inflammation of the lungs in which the space where air should be is filled with pus. Because addicts have poor health and a weakened immune system, bacterial pneumonia and tuberculosis are common among addicts.

Endocarditis, an inflammation of the heart, is found among injecting drug users. Bacteria attack the inner lining of the heart, particularly around the heart's valves. This causes the valves to function so poorly that the heart itself fails.

Also common among addicts are yeast infections. The organism *Candida albicans* causes the disease known as thrush, which is characterized by fevers and chills, and sometimes an eye disease that can lead to blindness.

Addicts are at high risk for contracting hepatitis B and C— diseases that inflame the liver. The symptoms of hepatitis are fatigue, pain in the upper abdomen, feelings of sickness, and general ill health as well as the characteristic yellowy eyes of jaundice. The hepatitis virus can be transmitted by sharing contaminated needles and by engaging in unprotected sexual intercourse—the same way in which HIV, the virus that causes AIDS, is known to spread.

AIDS AND NEEDLE EXCHANGE PROGRAMS

Acquired immunodeficiency syndrome (AIDS), the most severe and life-threatening result of HIV (human immunodeficiency virus) infection, involves the destruction of a person's immune system and the development of cancers and infections that the body can no longer fight off. The HIV virus has a very long incubation period and may be present seven or more years before active symptoms of opportunistic disease appear. Early symptoms may include a persistent rash or lesion, unexplained weight loss, persistent night sweats or low-grade fever, persistent diarrhea or fatigue, swollen lymph glands, depression, or states of mental confusion.

The first cases of AIDS were diagnosed in 1981. Since then, 612,000 Americans have been reported as having the disease, according to the Centers for Disease Control and Prevention. This number does not include the estimated 275,000 Americans who are unaware they are HIV-positive. By 1997, 397,258 people had died from AIDS.

HIV can be transmitted only by blood or semen. The trace amount of blood left on a hypodermic needle is sufficient to transmit the virus. Over one-third of AIDS cases diagnosed since 1988 are the direct result of needle sharing, sexual contact with injecting drug users, or transmission in utero or at birth from an injecting drug user-infected mother to her baby.

It is not surprising that the highest incidence of HIV infection in the United States among injecting drug users is in areas such as New York City, where there is a tradition of needle sharing and where "shooting galleries" (places where users can rent or share "works") are commonly found. In other areas, such as San Francisco, where users do not share needles or keep the same "shooting partners" over a long period of time, the percentage of infection is lower.

The need to reduce HIV transmission among and from injecting drug users led to the creation of needle exchange programs. Their objective is to trade used needles and syringes for new ones.

The first needle exchange program opened in Amsterdam, Netherlands, in 1984. Programs in other European countries soon followed. In the United States, needle exchange programs are highly controversial. In contrast to Europe, where the health consequences of drug use are the main concern, in the United States the criminality of drug use and its punishment take center stage.

Although by 1999, there were 113 needle exchange programs active in 80 U.S. cities in 30 states, "paraphernalia" laws still exist in 46 states and the District of Columbia, and prescription laws are in place in ten states. "Paraphernalia laws" make possession and distribution of drug-taking equipment (including hypodermic needles) illegal. Prescription laws make possession of needles illegal without a doctor's prescription.

Those who oppose needle exchange programs argue that their legalization would send the wrong message, especially to the young, about the morality of drug use. They believe that providing clean needles would encourage drug use. However, the contrary seems to be true. The Mersey region of England where needle exchange programs were first implemented has the lowest number of HIV-positive drug users in England and the highest rate of drug users receiving treatment. In one of England's largest cities, Liverpool, the HIV-infection rate for injecting drug users is 0.1 percent compared with 60 percent in New York City.

Within the United States, the rate of HIV infection among

HIV AND HEROIN

HIV has been reported among injecting drug users (IDUs) in 60 countries on all continents except Antarctica. HIV spreads among a population of IDUs at a disturbing speed. When it was introduced in Edinburgh, Scotland, the HIV virus infected over 40 percent of the local IDUs within two years; in Manipur, India it infected over 50 percent of users within one year; and in Bangkok, Thailand the percentage of HIV-infected IDUs increased from two percent to over 40 percent in less than a year.

In the United States, a study conducted by the Centers for Disease Control and Prevention traced the spread of HIV from one single IDU prisoner diagnosed with AIDS to 50 of the 142 people linked to him directly or through someone else by sex or needle-sharing in the previous months. Twenty-four of the infected 50 did not know they had the virus when they were contacted.

injecting drug users entering treatment from states that have prescription laws is 15 percent, compared with three percent from states without such laws.

In 1997, a panel of the National Institutes of Health agreed that since the needle exchange programs were created, there has been a "reduction in risk behavior as high as 80 percent in IDUs (injecting drug users), with estimates of a 30 percent reduction of HIV." Another advantage of the programs is that they reduce the amount of used equipment discarded in the community where anyone can touch it and become a potential victim. As the example of the Mersey region indicates, needle exchange programs also serve as a bridge between drug addicts and drug treatment.

The ideology behind needle exchange programs is not to condone or encourage drug use but to reduce the individual and social harm associated with injecting the drug. This is why its policy is termed "harm reduction" or "harm minimization." Dirk Chase Eldredge argues in his book, *Ending the War on Drugs*, that even though injecting drugs is destructive and distasteful, it should not be deserving of a death sentence.

4

Trends and Attitudes

WHO USES HEROIN

With only five percent of the world's population, the United States consumes 60 percent of its illicit drugs. This means that tens of millions of people in America either have used or are using illegal drugs. Fortunately, not all these people are the drug-crazed, gun-toting thugs we read about, ready to rob or kill for their next fix. Most of them are ordinary citizens with jobs and mortgages and children in Little League. They take drugs occasionally or even regularly, but only for recreational purposes, and their lives are not subordinate to the substance.

A list of people arrested for buying drugs in a police sweep in Massachusetts in July 1993 reads as follows: a student hairdresser, a fast-food cook, a computer salesman, a registered nurse, a firefighter, a truck driver, two roofers, a machine operator, a carpenter, a telephone lineman, and a dry wall installer. Although this list cannot be considered a scientific survey, it shows that people from a wide variety of professions, and with no criminal background, may use drugs.

This does not mean that using drugs, especially heroin, is safe. In the United States alone, 3,000 to 4,000 users die annually of heroin overdose—from heroin alone or combined with other drugs. Heroin use, by itself or because of the addict's recklessness that leads him or her to share needles or engage in unprotected

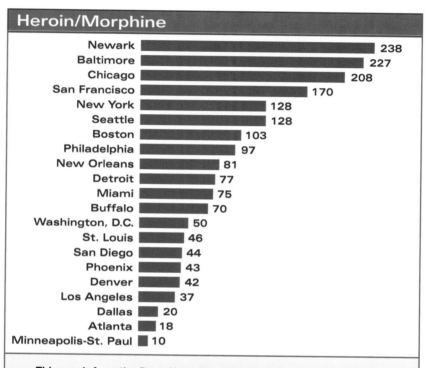

Heroin/Morphine

Newark	238
Baltimore	227
Chicago	208
San Francisco	170
New York	128
Seattle	128
Boston	103
Philadelphia	97
New Orleans	81
Detroit	77
Miami	75
Buffalo	70
Washington, D.C.	50
St. Louis	46
San Diego	44
Phoenix	43
Denver	42
Los Angeles	37
Dallas	20
Atlanta	18
Minneapolis-St. Paul	10

This graph from the Drug Abuse Warning Network ranks the number of heroin-related emergency room visits per every 100,000 people for major metropolitan areas across the United States. Since the majority of drug trafficking and abuse takes place in poverty-stricken urban areas, it follows that the majority of emergency room visits for drug-related illnesses will occur in these same areas.

sex, increases the risk of AIDS and other infectious diseases with lethal results.

Contrary to popular belief promoted by drug campaigns, not everyone who tries heroin will become addicted to it. Regardless of the good intentions of these campaigns—to keep children away from drugs—this information is not accurate and must be challenged to avoid further damage. Eventually, children learn by experience or through peers that addiction is not the inevitable outcome of drug use and will reject any further, and truthful, information about drugs they may receive.

Drug researchers estimate that there are about 800,000 hard-core heroin users in the United States. Although they account for 20 percent of all drug users, they consume about 75 percent of all the heroin and are responsible for most of the criminal behavior associated with heroin use.

Who are these hard-core users? Certainly plenty of affluent Americans are addicted to drugs; yet the government's annual National Household Survey on Drug Abuse reveals no great epidemic of chronic drug use among the middle class. The hard-core users are mainly poor, unemployed members of minority groups.

It is not their ethnicity, but their environment that makes these minority groups more susceptible to addiction. Data indicate that most heroin traffic and heroin use take place in the ghettos of the large cities. Since these areas are mostly populated by African Americans, Puerto Ricans, and Mexican Americans, these groups are at special risk. In all, men seem to develop opioid dependence more often than women do; the ratio of men to women in treatment programs is about three to one.

The difference between hard-core users and casual users—also called "chippers"—lies mainly in the way they use the drug. Chippers take heroin to reach euphoria; addicts take it to avoid pain. Chippers follow rituals; they take drugs at social occasions or to unwind on weekends. They budget their drug money and avoid slighting their responsibilities.

Addicts use drugs for their own sake. Any time is a good time. Taking drugs interferes with their jobs, families, and lives. They abandon other activities. Their life revolves around drugs.

Both hard-core users and casual users use the same drug, but the outcome is vastly different. So it seems that the difference among abstinence, occasional use, and addiction or dependence is a matter of personal choice.

WHY PEOPLE USE HEROIN
To Escape Reality

It is in the nature of all mammals, including human beings, to use substances or to engage in activities that will alter their minds. Free-roaming animals gladly intoxicate themselves when they have the chance: cats with catnip, cattle with locoweed, squirrels with pine cone seeds. In Vietnam, water buffaloes under the stress of air-raid attacks headed for the coca leaves and started chewing on them. Children make themselves dizzy by twirling around, and there are hints that chimpanzees do the same with dance. So, like the scorpion that drowned after stinging the frog that carried it across the river, humans take drugs because it is in their nature to do so.

In the particular case of heroin, the "pleasure" is both an absence—an escape from pain—and a positive reaction—a feeling of well-being. Taking this search for pleasure a step farther, humans also take drugs in the hope that they will enhance their creativity or productivity. Artists, writers, and musicians have done so throughout history. Although it may be argued that this approach has worked for some, it has brought tragedy to many.

Because humans, unlike animals, are not driven solely by instincts, it seems logical to expect more restraint in their use of drugs. After all, humans know that using heroin will jeopardize their health, and since it is an illegal drug, it will jeopardize their freedom as well. Nevertheless, statistics show this knowledge is not enough to deter everyone.

Curiosity and Peer Pressure

Illicit drug use usually starts as a casual event involving no more forethought than the first drink of cola. For many first-time users, the process flows naturally from knowing about heroin to knowing someone who uses it, to trying it themselves.

Contrary to popular belief, it is usually a friend who introduces the user to the drug and not the dark evil figure of the unknown "pusher." Sometimes the friend is both a user and a dealer. Heroin is, after all, a profitable though illicit business.

Madison's dad came straight from work to bail her out of jail. Madison thought to herself that it was just her kind of luck—to get busted on her first time trying heroin. As soon as they got in the car, the lecture started. Madison leaned back against the cold leather of the car seat, nodded from time to time, but wasn't really paying attention.

"No, Dad. Of course I didn't know they would be doing drugs."

"No, Dad. I will never do it again."

"Yes, Dad. I know you wouldn't have let me go to the party. But Mom said yes, and you weren't there."

"Yes, I know how important your meeting was, and that if I fool around, it reflects bad on you."

Madison's mind drifted back to the previous night and the incredible feeling that rushed through her body after that white powder went up her nose. The peace, the void, the humming. All her problems gone, no more hurting, no more worries.

Madison's dad was still going strong on his speech.

"I hope you have learned your lesson, Madison. I hope from now on you will remember what's important in life."

Madison nodded and closed her eyes, but felt all the trouble was worth it.

Although Madison felt at peace using heroin, she may not know that heroin always causes more problems than it solves. One out of every six heroin users suffers depression—a statistic that jumps to one out of every three for heroin addicts trying to quit. For teens, heroin has the added disadvantage of interfering with normal physical and emotional developmental processes.

Dealers do not need to give away heroin; they have enough buyers as it is.

Apart from curiosity, the determining factor in trying heroin is the group of people whom the nonuser hangs out with. Being in an environment where drugs are routinely used will put pressure on the nonuser to do the same. The urge to conform and be accepted, so-called "peer pressure," is a strong motivator not only among teenagers, but also among people in their 20s and even in their 30s.

Continued use of heroin may be related to personal frustrations, but these have nothing to do with the first try. Most drug users drifted into taking heroin through mild peer-group pressure and chance and, with few exceptions, within a few years of their twentieth birthday.

Rite of Passage and the Need to Rebel

Adolescence is a confusing time, a time of many physical, cognitive, social, and emotional changes. Although most children adapt to these changes in healthy ways, others go through a period of turmoil and engage in deviant behaviors, of which taking drugs is but one.

For adolescents who come from a predominantly white culture, heroin use can be seen as a form of rebellion. As Humberto Fernandez writes in his book *Heroin*:

> Driving to the city, braving the dangers of a drug neighborhood, and making it back home to the suburbs all validate the person's courage and ability while displaying reckless disregard for the conventions of society. Each drug-seeking episode is another opportunity to outsmart the police, feel the thrill of the hunt, and come back alive to feel the high, which in and of itself is ample justification.

The lure of the drug subculture can be difficult to resist for the young. As described by Danny Sugerman, the agent for Jim

Morrison's rock group, The Doors, in his book *Wonderland Avenue*, it is indeed a fascinating life. This life of glamour and excess, of nightclubbing and drugs doesn't last forever, though. In the afterword to his book, Sugerman tells us what happens to the people whose story he has just told. Sixteen of the 29 characters were dead, two were in jail, one was living in a wheelchair, blind and unable to speak, her left side paralyzed by an overdose, and one was in a recovery program for the third time—not exactly a glamorous tale.

For people of color living in ghettos, the story is quite different. Because for decades, they have been denied the opportunity to compete in the dominant culture owing to poor education and racism in hiring practices, some have created their own economy based on dealing and using drugs. Young people growing up in this subculture have been exposed to drugs all their lives. For them, using heroin is but a rite of passage to becoming an adult, a way to prove to their peers they are old enough and tough enough to handle the hardest of drugs: heroin.

Glamour and Fashion

News about celebrities being arrested for drug possession or dying from an overdose works two ways on the minds of the public. On the one hand, it is a warning against the danger of drug use. On the other, it glamorizes drugs.

The 1994 death by suicide of 27-year-old Kurt Cobain, heroin addict and leader of the rock group Nirvana, is an example of the glamorization of drugs. All major magazines covered his death, lamenting "Cobain's pain" as symbolic of America's youth. As critic Frank Rich wrote, "The sound that (came) from his voice and his shrieking, feedback-choked guitar is the piercingly authentic cry of a child in torment." In his death, he became a hero for disenchanted young people who, like the 20-year-old student quoted in the *New York Times* believe, "He helped open people's eyes to our struggles."

A celebrity's well-publicized drug problem may serve as a warning to fans, but may also be seen as glamorous. As Kurt Cobain showed the world through his heroin-fueled downward spiral that led to suicide, heroin use is not glamorous, but rather, painfully destructive to the user.

Watching the movie *Sid and Nancy* was what prompted Nikki, one of the young women interviewed in Marc Miller's article in *Mademoiselle*, to try heroin. While the movie follows the love affair of Sid Vicious, bassist of the British band the Sex Pistols, and his girlfriend Nancy Spungeon and their love of heroin, it does nothing to glamorize heroin.

On the contrary, the movie describes with painstaking detail the growing desperation and shrinking prospects of heroin users.

According to Marc Miller's article, Nikki is not the only one taking heroin to follow the fashion. Apparently, a new generation of young professional women started using heroin at the beginning of the 1990s just because doing so was "hot." As Julia, a 30-year-old assistant photographer, explains, "The trendiness is the real peril, because anything new is tantalizing and this (heroin use) is considered new again."

The fashion industry may also have contributed to this trend by introducing the so-called "heroin-chic" in models— models so emaciated they seem to be on heroin.

This wave of heroin use could have been predicted from observing the cocaine and crack epidemic of the 1980s. As far back as 1885, cocaine and opiate epidemics have succeeded one another, each relieving the chronic problems of the last. Cocaine epidemics tend to be fast and short, accelerated by binge use. Cocaine cannot be taken for long periods of time because it burns the user out. After a cocaine epidemic, an epidemic of a sedative substance—like alcohol or heroin—will follow.

In contrast to the cocaine epidemics, heroin epidemics progress slowly. It takes an average of three to ten years for a user to go from regular use to treatment or arrest. Many heroin users of today are old-timers from the last epidemic of the 1970s, hard-core users who are in and out of rehab programs and/or jail. But another wave of heroin users (like the women described in Marc Miller's article) started at the beginning of the 1990s, pushed by the higher quality and lower prices of the heroin that hit the streets—the higher quality that allowed the user to snort it and avoid the fear of using the needle.

Whether the number of people using heroin is still rising

or is starting to decline is hard to tell. But the explosion of HIV infection among injection drug users makes this wave of heroin even more dangerous.

HEROIN AND THE ADDICTIVE PERSONALITY

"I started shooting up again. I don't know why."

People start taking heroin out of curiosity because it is available or fashionable, or because they want to change their mood. The reasons why people become addicted are more complex. As the lives of chippers demonstrate, drugs do

HEROIN USE IN THE UNITED STATES

According to the 1998 National Household Survey on Drug Abuse, an estimated 2.4 million people have used heroin at some time in their lives—130,000 of them within the month preceding the survey. In 1997, there were 81,000 new heroin users. A large proportion of these new users were smoking, snorting, or sniffing heroin, and most (87 percent) were under age 26, which was up from 61 percent in 1992.

The 1998 Drug Abuse Warning Network reported that 14 percent of all drug-related hospital emergency department episodes in the 21 metropolitan areas surveyed involved heroin. Between 1991 and 1996, heroin-related emergency department episodes doubled in the general population from 35,898 to 73,846. Among 12- to 17-year-olds, these episodes nearly quadrupled. The National Institute on Drug Abuse's Community Epidemiology Work Group, in its June 2000 survey, reports that injecting is on an upward trend among younger heroin users in Baltimore, Boston, Minneapolis/ St. Paul, Newark, New York City, and Seattle. In Boston, Chicago, Denver, Miami, and Washington, D.C., snorting seems to be increasing and is often the starting route for new users.

not force a dreary outcome on the user. The addict's desire for a limited life seems to lie within.

As far back as the 1920s, Dr. Lawrence Kolb, the first medical director of the Public Health Service Narcotic Hospital in Lexington, Kentucky, wrote that heroin addicts were thrill seekers, people trying to overcome feelings of inferiority. Heroin gave them a short relief of their problems, making them feel peaceful and euphoric, at least for a while.

The facts that opioid dependence does not develop in everyone who takes heroin and that most addicts seem to share certain traits suggest that certain persons may have a greater susceptibility to becoming addicted. They have what in medical terms is called an "addictive personality."

The characteristics of the addictive personality have not been clearly defined, but clinical and other studies point to three personality problems that seem to increase susceptibility.

> First, chronic emotional distress, such as depression, tension, anxiety, anger, is relieved by opioid drugs, and this relief probably prompts repeated use of the drug.
>
> Second, impaired capacity to regulate emotional distress increases the urgency of the need for relief.
>
> Third, an antisocial attitude makes it easy for the person to perform the illegal actions needed for regular illicit opioid use.
>
> *Encyclopedia of Drugs, Alcohol*
> *and Addictive Behavior*

These personality problems seem to originate partly from a genetic inheritance and partly from an adverse psychosocial experience.

According to the traditionalist school of addiction, all forms of addiction stem from the baby's first year of life and the quality of care received during that period. When the mother is unable to give adequate care to the baby—for instance, if they live in a war zone, or if the mother is the only provider and she is worried about getting food, paying the rent, and struggling to get by—the baby may develop an addictive personality when he or she grows up.

Both the fact that most heroin users come from dysfunctional families and also that many addicts describe the heroin high as "warm" all over or as a rush of warmth that brings to mind the way a baby looks when breastfeeding, seem to give credibility to this theory. In this sense, what the addict is seeking in the heroin high are the nurturing moments he never had of being held in his mother's arms and made to feel the world was a safe and warm place.

Other addicts take heroin to escape a life without a job or other source of interest or excitement. They may feel lonely, inferior, or incapable of competing in society, and wish to remain in the heroin subculture where, at least, they feel they have an identity, even if it is to be "a junkie." Heroin also gives their life a purpose: to get money to buy heroin, to find heroin, to inject it. In their own way, addicts are very industrious people. For some people, obtaining drugs is a game, a way of eluding their responsibilities, a way of avoiding life.

Adolescents are especially vulnerable. Heroin can help them to postpone taking charge of their lives. While they are high, they avoid responsibilities without feelings of guilt. Eventually what may have started as escape or rebellion against society becomes slavery to a chemical substance. This creates a new set of problems.

TRENDS IN HEROIN USE

Teens consider drugs the single most important problem young people face today.

According to the 1998 national survey made in schools by

the Center on Addiction and Substance Abuse (CASA), the awareness of illegal drugs is widespread:

- Two out of five middle school students and two out of three high school students know a friend or classmate who has used acid, cocaine, or heroin.

- Eight percent of 12-year-olds know a drug dealer at school; by the time they reach 17, more than half (56 percent) do.

- More that one-third (37 percent) of older teens (15- to 17-year-olds) have personally seen drugs sold on school grounds, as have 16 percent of 12- to 14-year-olds.

- Twenty-six percent of teens say they could buy hard drugs such as acid, cocaine, or heroin within one day.

- The transition from age 12 to 13 marks the most dramatic increase in a kid's exposure to drugs and a decisive shift in attitude about drugs and parental involvement in their lives.

Between ages 12 and 13:

- The percentage of teens who say they know a student at their school who sells illegal drugs almost triples—from 8 to 22 percent.

- A 13-year-old is almost three times more likely to know a teen who uses acid, cocaine, or heroin than a 12-year-old, and three times more likely to be able to buy acid, cocaine or heroin.

- The number of students (age 12 to 13) who say they would not report a fellow student they personally saw using illegal drugs nearly triples from 15 to 42 percent.

The survey also found a severe disconnection between the perception of principals, teachers, and students on the drug issue. For instance, 66 percent of students say their

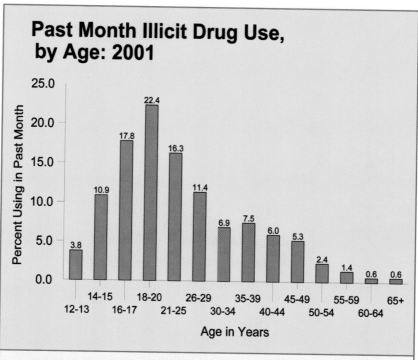

Past Month Illicit Drug Use, by Age: 2001

This graph from the National Household Survey on Drug Abuse shows the percentage of people in various age groups who used illicit (illegal) drugs—including heroin—in 2001. Drug use increases steadily during teen years, peaking at age 20. Similar statistics have been reported by the Center on Addiction and Substance Abuse and the 2001 Monitoring the Future Study.

school is *not* drug-free, compared with 11 percent of principals and 35 percent of teachers. Only 15 percent of high school principals say the drug problem is getting worse, whereas 41 percent of teachers and 51 percent of students believe this to be the case.

Another survey, the 2001 Monitoring the Future Study (MTF) conducted by the University of Michigan's Institute for Social Research and funded by the National Institute on Drug Abuse, National Institutes of Health, reports that heroin use declined from 2000 to 2001 among tenth and twelfth graders. For tenth graders, past year use decreased from 1.4 to 0.9 percent; for twelfth graders it was down from 1.5 to 0.9 percent.

In addition, long-term heroin use declined for both these grades. This decrease in overall heroin use among tenth and twelfth graders resulted largely from a decrease in use of the drug without a needle (i.e., snorting or smoking it).

This year's decrease in heroin use among twelfth graders reverses an increase in use of the drug in this grade between 1999 and 2000, which brought it to the highest level in the history of the survey; the new rate for 2001, 0.9 percent for past year use, is the lowest since 1994.

In summation, the 2001 MTF survey marks the fifth year in a row that illicit drug use among eighth, tenth, and twelfth graders remained stable or, in some cases, decreased. The rates of heroin use decreased notably among tenth and twelfth graders. In another front, the twelfth graders' disapproval of using heroin once or twice without a needle declined from 94.0 percent in 2000 to 91.7 percent in 2001.

THE WANDERJAHR

Drug use in adolescents is a serious problem. Yet, let us remember that although water buffaloes chew on coca leaves when under stress, they return to their previous activities when the danger disappears. As our politicians can testify, using drugs when young does not stop you from running for office or even from becoming president.

Maybe children must reject the world before they grow to accept it. As Norman Spinrad reminds us in *Child of Fortune*, to get to adulthood we must endure the *wanderjahr*, "the eternal journey from childhood to maturity through the wondrous and terrible chaos of the region between."

[The wanderjahr] is a necessary passage that takes many forms, a passage through a world that existed "outside, within, and as often as not in opposition to" society. To (this world) was drawn both the best and the worst of a culture's youth—the dreamers and the rebels, the idealists and the psychopaths, the artistic and the indolent, the seekers after vice and the seekers after enlightment.

Some journeyed a while in the realm of chaos and emerged once more as history's movers and shapers. Some passed through their *wanderjahr* and grew only old. Some were lost forever. A few remained young forever until the day they died.

5

Heroin Addiction

Pleasure is an "insatiable" drive in all humans that can be fulfilled in different ways. Because most addicts lead a life so lacking in meaning and purpose, they don't know this craving can be reached through means other than the "high" that drugs give them. Dr. Roy Matthews, head of Duke University Medical Center's Alcohol and Addiction Program, describes the correlation between pleasure and the nature of addiction in regard to the heroin addict:

> Drug abuse is not a problem with drugs, it's a problem with pleasure. . . . Pleasure is the basis of addiction, and it would seem pleasure is a solution to addiction.

Humberto Fernandez writes in his book *Heroin*:

> (For the addict) to stop using heroin is to take away the social network, identity, and the one thing that makes life easier to bear. Many addicts refer to heroin as their medication. When they are in withdrawal they "need to be cured." When you take away heroin from an addict, you often have a person who feels insecure, inferior, ashamed, and ill equipped to negotiate his or her way in the world. Poor social skills, lack of education, and the stigma of being branded an addict—a person with an incurable disease—add to the burden. It is not surprising that so few seek treatment when faced with these choices. [. . .]
>
> For those who seek recovery it is essential to fill the empty holes in their psyches that heroin once occupied. . . . In essence, heroin addicts must restructure their subculture and replace destructive habits and behaviors with healthy ones in order to recover.

While simplistic slogans like "Just Say No" may not work for high school students, some of the harder-hitting ads sponsored by the Partnership of a Drug Free America may. In a commercial designed to show the reality of heroin addiction, a young woman smashes an egg with a frying pan to show "this is your brain on heroin," and then proceeds to destroy her entire kitchen—dishes, wall clock, counters—to demonstrate what happens to a heroin user's friends, family, and future.

If an addict is to stay off heroin, he or she must find another "meaning in life," a positive drive that will displace the need for the drug. This shift of focus may be achieved through education or through a spiritual experience, a dramatic change in his or her life, the participation in a 12-step program, or other pharmacological/psychological treatment.

EDUCATION AND PREVENTION

Education works. The number of people smoking cigarettes in the United States dropped from 42.3 percent in 1965 to 25.4 percent in 1990. It dropped when people learned through a truthful educational campaign how harmful cigarette smoking really is and, of their own free will, chose not to smoke.

A similar approach might work with drugs. For a drug education policy to succeed, it should give the information in a realistic way and allow children to develop their own opinions about drugs and whether or not to use them. "Drug education for our children, even our young children, must be thoughtful, verifiable, reasonable, and practical—or it will fail," Judge James P. Gray writes.

Unfortunately, in America the Drug-Free Schools and Communities Act prohibits the use of federal funds for programs that do not clearly state that using drugs is wrong and harmful. This means that only one point of view is allowed. In this sense, the purpose of drug education is not to inform but to elicit a specific response—abstinence. The problem with this approach is that, given no choice, children feel bullied and tend to resist further information.

Simplistic slogans like "I believe in a drug-free America" or "Just Say No" may work for elementary school students, but teenagers need a more realistic approach. Even fourth graders realized that by sharpening down pencils with the words "It's not cool to do drugs" written on them, the saying changed to "cool to do drugs" and eventually "do drugs."

Of course, everyone would agree that drug use is risky, harmful, and unattractive and that in the best of worlds, total abstinence should be the goal. In this world, though, and starting in adolescence, many people will start experimenting with all kinds of risk-taking behaviors, drugs among them. As one student put it, "I did not take mescaline because I went to Harvard, met Timothy Leary, rebelled against my parents, was amotivated, or sought escape from reality. I took it because I was a normal American teenager whose curiosity had survived thirteen years of American education."

By preaching zero tolerance, once this behavior starts no further communication is possible, and young people are left to fend for themselves in the most confusing period of their lives. If not schools, at least parents should have an open discussion about drugs with their children and stress to them that their safety is the most important thing.

The importance of having a family member or friend to depend on is worth emphasizing. A survey from the National Longitudinal Study on Adolescence Health among 12,118 teenagers found that teenagers who felt close to their parents and siblings, teachers, and classmates were less likely to engage in risky behaviors.

SELF-CURE: THE EBENEZER SCROOGE EFFECT

Not everyone who starts taking heroin on a daily basis continues using it indefinitely. Studies suggest that heroin abuse is typically a young person's habit, a habit most people outgrow as they mature. Most users are young, not because of a higher death rate among them, but because most people stop taking the drug within 10 years of first use. Data from one study that followed high school students from 1971 through young adulthood shows that 73 percent of those who had tried heroin had stopped by 1980, and another eight percent stopped by 1983.

The reasons why most people quit using drugs are related to the fact that drug use depends not only on the pharmacological properties of the drug, but also on the set and the setting. Set is the psychological state the user brings to the experience. Setting refers to the social and environmental conditions in which the drug is taken.

In a clear example of set and setting, during the Vietnam War many American soldiers got addicted to narcotic drugs. After returning home in 1975, most of them gave up using them altogether. When they started using drugs, they had been scared, fighting in a foreign country, with plenty of time and money to spend, and narcotic drugs were cheap and available. As soon as they were back with their families in their own environment, the need for drugs was no longer there, and most quit.

In a reverse example, many drug addicts stop using heroin when in jail. By the time they are released, they are no longer addicted. Once they are back on their "home turf" they return to their old ways, and start shooting up again.

Self-cure without treatment, sometimes called "the Ebenezer Scrooge effect" after the protagonist of Charles Dickens's *A Christmas Carol,* can also be achieved by a religious conversion or even a traumatic crisis like a drug-related arrest or the death of a friend from overdose. In all such cases of self-cure, people leave addiction when they develop reasons to avoid it. Or, as Stanton Peele writes, ending addiction involves "development of internal capacities—interests, joys, competencies—to counteract the desire for escape and self-obliteration."

THE NEED FOR TREATMENT

For most heroin users, what started as a pleasurable, social activity becomes an all-consuming habit. When this happens and their lives become a continued struggle to avoid the withdrawal symptoms and the craving, most addicts want a way out.

Because those who quit on their own usually have no further contact with the drug culture, most users do not have a role model to show them self-cure is possible. Many fear the symptoms of withdrawal that they will suffer when they stop taking heroin, and they find it easier to give in and medicate themselves with the next "fix" than go through this unpleasant period.

A detoxification program can help heroin users go through withdrawal. But detoxification alone is usually not enough. Evidence of this goes back to the 1930s when the first attempt to cure addicts was made by the U.S. government. To do so, all the heroin addicts in federal custody were sent to the Public Health Service Narcotic Hospital in Lexington, Kentucky. In this facility, no drugs were available. When these "cured" people were released and went back to their homes, most turned back to heroin once more, proving that detoxification alone does not work.

Treatment for heroin dependency must address not only the physical signs of addiction, but also the craving for the drug and other psychological, social, and legal problems addicts usually have. When all these issues are addressed, the chances of success are as high for those who enter the program voluntarily as for those forced into it by relatives or as a condition for staying out of jail.

There are several types of treatment that differ in the setting they are offered—inpatient or outpatient—and also in the relative role that psychological and pharmacological approaches have in treatment. At one end of the spectrum is the therapeutic community where patients receive only counseling and psychological treatment in a residential setting and the 12-steps programs. At the other end are the methadone maintenance clinics where the emphasis is in daily oral administration of methadone, whereas counseling and psychotherapy are secondary.

In the same way that people use drugs in different ways and for different reasons, no single treatment program is effective for everyone. The choice of treatment depends on each individual person.

DETOXIFICATION

The term "detoxification" is a misnomer stemming from a discredited theory that the withdrawal syndrome was caused by toxins and that treatment consisted of purging the body of these toxins. According to Lipton and Maranda in *Treatment of Opiate Addiction with Methadone: A Counselor's Manual*, (p. 39), a more accurate term would be 'supervised withdrawal,' since the procedure consists of ameliorating the withdrawal syndrome.

When a heroin user enters a detoxification program, he or she is given a pharmacological agent, usually methadone, to alleviate symptoms of withdrawal.

Methadone is a weak-acting synthetic opiate agonist, which imitates the action of an opiate and reduces symptoms of heroin withdrawal but does not generate euphoria. Methadone is usually given orally once every 24 hours. The goal of this treatment is to gradually lower the dose from 25 milligrams—its usual starting point—to zero over a period of seven days.

Sometimes the nonopioid clonidine is used instead of methadone. Clonidine suppresses the physical symptoms of withdrawal, but does not help with the more subjective ones, such as lethargy, restlessness, and dysphoria. Despite its side effects of low blood pressure, sedation, and blurry vision that make it unpleasant to take, the fact that clonidine is not an opioid makes it a good choice as a first step to get the patient onto naltrexone.

Naltrexone is an opiate antagonist, which binds more strongly than heroin to the same brain receptors. When an addict takes naltrexone, it expels the heroin from the opioid receptors and produces sudden and severe withdrawal symptoms. A combination treatment of clonidine to suppress the intensity of withdrawal symptoms and naltrexone to accelerate the pace of withdrawal has been used for rapid detoxification.

Naltrexone is also used after detoxification to prevent addicts from relapsing into heroin use. Because naltrexone binds to opioid receptors in the user's brain more tightly than does heroin, heroin cannot produce its characteristic "high." Contrary to rumors circulating among addicts, naltrexone does not suppress other "natural highs."

A typical detoxification program lasts three weeks. During this time, the patient meets not only with the nurse who provides the medication, but with a counselor as well. The role of the counselor is to support the patients through the discomforts of withdrawal and to provide information on the different types of treatments available to them.

METHADONE MAINTENANCE

When heroin addicts come into treatment for the first time, they are put through detoxification and possibly put on naltrexone maintenance. If they have the support of family, have good jobs, and have strong motivation, naltrexone

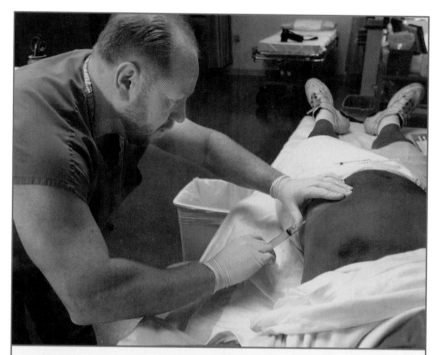

The doctor shown here is implanting a pellet of naltrexone into a heroin addict's stomach to initiate rapid detoxification. By binding tightly to opiate receptors, naltrexone effectively inhibits heroin already in the addict's system from binding to these receptors. Naltrexone continues to bind to the opiate receptors after implantation, thereby preventing the rewarding "high" the addict would normally feel if they were to lapse back into drug use.

maintenance is usually effective at keeping them away from heroin. Younger addicts and adolescents are also encouraged to try no-methadone approaches to avoid methadone addiction. Only patients who have failed previous detoxification programs and pregnant women (to avoid the adverse effects of sudden withdrawal on the unborn child) are candidates for methadone maintenance.

Patients on methadone maintenance receive a fixed dose of methadone on a regular basis to maintain their normal physiological state. The administration of methadone eliminates the

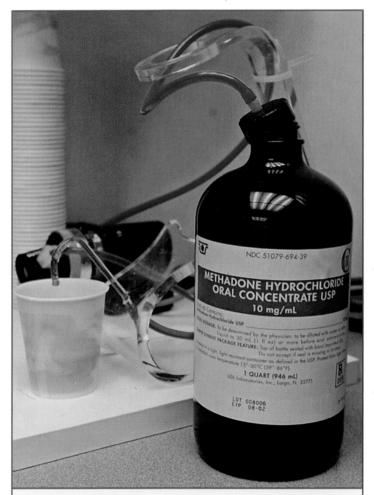

A patient's daily dose of methadone is dispensed into a small cup and ingested orally. Methadone is an opioid-like heroin, but has a much slower high producing onset (i.e., less intense) than heroin. Methadone maintenance curbs the addict's craving for heroin, but does not cure the addiction to the drug.

uncontrolled craving for heroin and allows the addict to lead a normal life.

Some detractors of methadone treatment believe it is only a way of substituting one opioid for another. However, methadone's effects have a slower onset than those of heroin, and methadone does not produce a high. Moreover, because it is an opioid, methadone increases the level of tolerance of the user to any opioid. This means that people on methadone maintenance will not get high if they take heroin.

An advantage of methadone maintenance is that heroin intake among addicts in treatment declines as does the criminal behavior because addicts don't need to steal to buy heroin. There is also a general improvement in the overall health of society since the transmission by needle sharing of HIV virus and other infectious diseases is reduced.

Nevertheless, methadone is a medication, not a cure for heroin addiction—a medication that most experts agree will not stop addiction. In fact, the current Food and Drug Administration regulations require methadone treatment to include other psychosocial services that will address the broader psychological, vocational, legal, social, and medical problems that heroin addicts usually have by the time they reach treatment.

Other medications used for maintenance treatment of heroin dependence are buprenorphine and LAAM (levo-alpha -acetylmethadol). Buprenorphine is a partial opioid agonist medication that is safe, even at high doses, and has less severe withdrawal symptoms than methadone when stopped.

LAAM is a long-acting analogue of methadone that is currently under investigation. It requires administration three times per week instead of daily, as methadone requires. Because the onset of LAAM's action is slow, a combination of methadone followed by LAAM treatment may work best.

THERAPEUTIC COMMUNITIES

Therapeutic communities are long-term (6- to 24-month) residential programs that provide treatment in a highly structured and hierarchical residential setting. The patient receives rewards or penalties for conduct, while he or she learns how to live without drugs by observing the behavior of peers and staff. As time passes, the patient is given more important jobs within the community until eventually he or she becomes a responsible member. Although these therapeutic communities have traditionally been run by their own interns, more recently, professionals with or without prior drug history provide managerial expertise and treatment.

Treatment programs modeled after therapeutic communities are also becoming popular in prison systems. Prisoners with drug abuse history are given the opportunity to join the program six to 12 months before their date of release. The rate of success is higher for those who continue the residential treatment after they are out of prison.

DRUG ABUSE COUNSELING

Drug abuse counseling is provided both in methadone maintenance and in outpatient community clinic programs. Counselors may be professionals with a college degree in counseling or ex-addicts who have personal experience with recovery from drug abuse.

Counselors have several roles. First, they check that the addict is not taking drugs. They do this by random urine tests and by searching the arms and the body for needle marks. Second, they help the addict to set step-by-step goals to go back to a normal life. Finally, they refer patients to other community helping agencies for other services as needed. For example, if the person is unemployed, he or she may be referred to an employment counseling service.

MOTIVATIONAL INCENTIVE THERAPY

The motivational incentive program is designed to stop heroin use for a while (3 to 6 months). The goal is to give counselors and addicts time to work on making the lifestyle changes necessary to stay off drugs for longer periods. This incentive program does this by offering an increasing number of points to the addict for each consecutive day the urine test is negative (the urine test is used to determine whether the addict is drug-free). If the patient has a relapse and the urine test is positive, the number of points is reset to the original number. The earned points translate into money the addict can use to pay rent or buy groceries or other retail items.

PSYCHOTHERAPY

Psychotherapy is a psychological treatment practiced by trained clinical psychologists, psychiatrists, and psychiatric social workers. It uses interpersonal skills to help patients to understand why they use heroin and to help them change this behavior. Psychotherapy can be done individually or in

DOES TREATMENT WORK?

Since the same drug treatment does not work for every addict, some people assume treatment never works and should be discontinued. Although many people do go in and out of treatment and all programs have a large number of dropouts, statistics show that one-third of those who stay for at least three months are still drug free one year later. Two-thirds remain drug free when they stay in treatment one year or longer.

Even if it takes many tries to reach total abstinence, treatment works. It works while the addict is on treatment. It works when the length of time between an addict's relapses increases with each treatment. It definitely works for society as a whole. An untreated drug abuser costs society $43,000 per year in social services, medical care, and crime. To keep that addict in jail costs about $40,000 per year, whereas to keep the person in a residential treatment costs an average of $16,500 per year.

groups. Group psychotherapy provides a context for mutual empathy, encouragement, and support among people with similar problems. The interaction among group members also helps to improve social skills.

The most common types of psychotherapy are psycho-dynamic therapy and cognitive-behavioral therapy.

Psychodynamic Therapy

In psychodynamic therapy, the belief is that to give up heroin, the patient must first resolve the psychological problems that cause drug use in the first place. Drug use is considered a symptom of the addict's underlying emotional problems or relationship difficulties. Because this treatment does not attempt to stop drug use directly, the patient must already be abstinent before starting.

Cognitive-Behavioral Therapy

Unlike psychodynamic therapy, cognitive-behavioral therapy tries to change behavior (heroin use) directly even when the causes of its use are unknown. The goal of the treatment is to teach patients the skills necessary to stop using heroin and stay drug-free. In each case, the therapist tries to understand the thoughts, behaviors, and environmental conditions that precede and follow heroin use and help the patient to change them or avoid them. For instance, patients and therapist may work together to devise strategies for avoiding drug-using friends and staying away from places in which the patient bought or used drugs in the past.

Apart from avoidance, the therapist also teaches the patients new skills to cope with high-risk situations. For example, if patients used heroin in times of stress, they can be taught relaxation techniques. If they have problems controlling their anger and use drugs after an angry confrontation, they can be taught to avoid anger-producing situations or they can be taught new self-statements to replace thoughts that precede feelings of anger (e.g., "It would be nice to get an A, but it is not the end of the world if I do not get it").

Family Therapy

Heroin abuse disrupts the family. On the other hand, most heroin addicts are raised in dysfunctional families and may replicate in their own personal and romantic relationship the maladaptive behavior patterns learned from their families. That is why it is important, especially for adolescents still living at home, to include the family in the treatment process.

According to the *Encyclopedia of Drugs, Alcohol & Addictive Behavior*,

> [The goal of family therapy is] to help the family to recognize maladaptive patterns of behavior, to learn better ways of solving family problems, to better understand each other's needs and concerns, and to identify and modify family interactions that may be helping to maintain drug use in the targeted family member.

SELF-HELP GROUPS

The first self-help group, Alcoholic Anonymous (AA), was created in 1935 by recovering alcoholics with the idea that alcoholics could help each other to abstain. Narcotic Anonymous (NA) and Methadone Anonymous (MA) are two new self-help groups that share the same principles of AA but are aimed at heroin addicts and people in methadone maintenance, respectively.

Members of self-help groups attend meetings regularly, sometimes even daily. At these meetings, members speak to each other about their drug use and drug-related problems and offer each other mutual advice and support.

The philosophy and goals of self-help groups are written in a book called *The 12 Steps to Recovery*. The book outlines

Madison waited for the door to close and ran upstairs. She quickly went through her dad's drawers, reassuring herself that she was not stealing—she'd return the money as soon as she got a summer job. Besides it's all his fault, she thought, since he's the one who cut her allowance just because her grades dropped. It wasn't like she failed anything, she just got a few Bs and a C.

And her mom was no better. "No more clothes until your grades go up."

Clothes, yeah right. Her mom didn't even notice that she hasn't bought clothes in ages. Spoiled, that's the problem. She told herself that her parents are totally spoiled because she always got straight As. Well, that was it. She had enough of being the perfect girl. Now, it was her turn to have some fun, and for that she needed money. Steve told her no more dope until she paid him back.

What kind of friend is he? She didn't even know why she hung out with him. She didn't need him—him or his stupid smack for that matter. It wasn't like she was hooked or anything. It's just that it had been a tough week and a little smoke would make her feel better. Smoke. That's it. Or maybe she would try shooting, that way she could make it stretch longer.

She smiled at her face in the mirror. "Madison, you are a genius," she told herself, as she put all the change she gathered into her pocket and dashed downstairs. "Today's graduation day—I shoot for the first time."

Madison probably doesn't realize how quickly she is sliding towards addiction. Heroin has become her primary focus. Things that once mattered—her grades, her clothes, her parents—have taken a backseat to getting her next fix. Instead of the bright future that awaits most graduates, Madison's "graduation day" to needle-use puts her on the fast track to heroin dependence.

a series of tasks that would promote abstinence and long-term recovery from alcohol or drug use. The first step necessary for recovery is for the person to admit having a problem with drugs or alcohol and admit the need for external help. The sources of help are a higher spiritual power and the other group members. From them, the addict gathers the spiritual strength necessary to stop drug use. Other changes in the addict's life include attendance at group meetings and concentration on the goal of abstinence summarized in AA's motto, "one day at a time." Usually, a new member is paired with a sponsor, someone who has been in the community for a long time, to guide him or her and to offer support in times of crisis.

The concepts of AA are included in many drug treatment programs, or, if not included, the patients are advised to join a self-help group.

Experience has shown that those who attend at least one month of residential drug treatment and continue to attend AA-type meetings regularly are almost twice as likely to remain off drugs than those who do not attend the follow-up support sessions.

6

Heroin and the Law

Heroin is an illegal drug in the United States. This means you can go to jail for possessing, selling, or using heroin. All illegal drugs under U.S. legislation are classified into five schedules by the Controlled Substance Act of 1970 according to their effects, medical use, and potential for abuse. Heroin is in Schedule I, which includes the drugs most strictly controlled.

The fact that heroin is illegal has not stopped its distribution but has had the unwanted consequence of making it more expensive. A kilogram (about two pounds) of heroin that costs about $85,000 coming into the United States can yield over 30,000 $10 bags in the street, with a net profit of more than $200,000.

For dealers, this means that the business is incredibly profitable. For the user, it means that heroin addiction is an expensive habit. For example, a once-rich Hollywood art dealer was convicted of planning several bank robberies to pay for his $800 a day drug addiction. In fact, stealing and prostitution are common among addicts—not because heroin has the direct effect of turning users into criminals, but because the need for money to buy drugs to satisfy their craving forces, or they allow it to force them, into crime.

"I had to move out of my home because I stole from my dad," a young man explains. "I live in an apartment with nothing in it now. I felt ashamed and embarrassed about stealing from my dad, but I

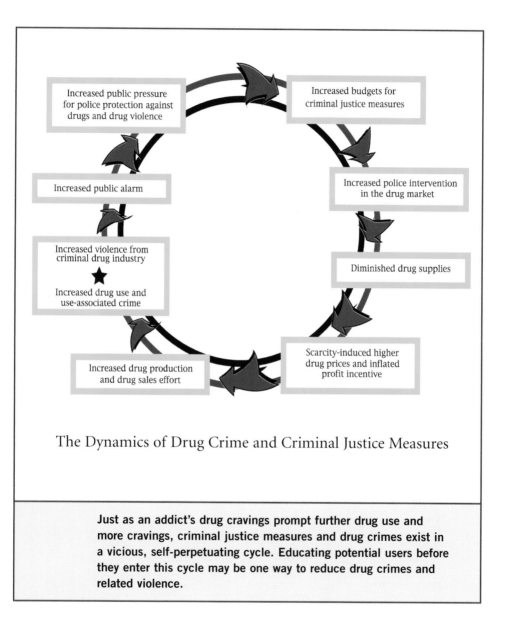

The Dynamics of Drug Crime and Criminal Justice Measures

Just as an addict's drug cravings prompt further drug use and more cravings, criminal justice measures and drug crimes exist in a vicious, self-perpetuating cycle. Educating potential users before they enter this cycle may be one way to reduce drug crimes and related violence.

had to score. If you need to score you'll do anything. I haven't seen my parents since."

Statistics show that drug users are responsible for at least 40 percent of all property crimes. That is about 8 million crimes per year and $6 billion in stolen property. To make matters worse, many crime victims are beaten and injured and 1,600 are murdered each year.

Using heroin often leads to arrest and prison records, which make finding a job more difficult after release. This pushes heroin users even farther into the drug culture. Heroin use also stimulates crime by forcing users into daily contact with the professional criminals who sell it. For some upper-class and middle-class teenagers driven by boredom, this can add an extra thrill to the heroin high. But it may be a deadly one.

For a poorly educated person from an inner city, whose employment outlook is bleak, the decision to deal drugs may seem like a good one to ensure a certain degree of economic prosperity. Drug dealing is a tough life, however. Drug dealers are professional criminals willing to murder competitors, informers, and police as needed. Shootings over territorial turfs or drug possession often end in deaths, sometimes of innocent bystanders.

In some areas, going to jail is so common that it is not a deterrent; on the contrary, it is considered a badge of honor. But life is prison is far from glamorous. So many people are prosecuted for drug offenses that prisons are overcrowded, and atrocities are committed on a regular basis. As Chief Judge Donald P. Lay of the U.S. Court of Appeals in St. Paul, Minnesota, writes:

> A few years ago, I visited a correctional institution in a southern state. A 19-year-old boy had just been sentenced for one year for possession of marijuana. He was received in their central processing unit, designed to hold 120 prisoners. At that time there were 465 prisoners incarcerated in small cells in a four-level building that afforded little ventilation and no recreational area.

The young man was sent to a psychological evalua-
tion unit. After two hours, they picked up his exam
papers and he had written only four words: "Help Me.
Help Me." Officials discovered that he had been put in a
small cell block containing four beds with 11 other
inmates who had sexually assaulted him for 48 hours,
every hour on the hour . . . "

ENFORCEMENT

For politicians in the 1960s, the solution to the heroin problem
seemed simple:

1. Stop the demand by prevention/education programs
   and by putting those who are already using heroin
   into treatment.

2. Stop the supply through interdiction, tough enforcement strategies, and incarceration of users and dealers.

To accomplish these objectives, both the number of
government agencies involved and the amount of money
spent on the war on drugs increased dramatically over the
following years:

- In 1969, eight agencies and four cabinet departments
  received drug-program funding.

- In 1993, 45 agencies and 21 cabinet departments
  received drug-program funding.

- In 1969, the total budget for federal drug-abuse
  programs was $81 million; for 2000, about
  $17.8 billion.

Yet, the number of addicts has also increased from 200,000
in 1915, the first year the first national control laws became
effective to over 800,000 in 2000. How is this possible?

Heroin trafficking generates huge profits and violent crime. These police officers from the Baltimore, Maryland, Police Department seized four kilograms of heroin, $100,000, and seven guns in one raid in 2001.

Money is one of the reasons. The heroin business is extremely profitable. Sales of heroin in the United States alone total more that the combined profits of the top 500 U.S. corporations and more than the budgets of many developing countries. This translates into very well-organized crime organizations around the world with money to spare for bribing whole governments.

Another reason is that heroin is easy to smuggle. The amount of illegal heroin that supplies the United Kingdom for one day would fit into a single shopping bag. As for the United States, a look at the map will give the answer. The United States shares a 2,500-mile-long land border with Mexico, over 3,000 miles with Canada, and to the east and west there is open ocean. Under these circumstances, an effective drug supply interdiction is virtually impossible.

The fact that heroin is easy to produce also contributes to the problem. American heroin users consume an estimated six tons of heroin each year. This may seem a daunting amount, but not if we consider that the 60 tons of opium required to produce that heroin are only two or three percent of the world-estimated production of opium in the last few years. By sheer power of numbers, the U.S. heroin users have a good chance of getting their supply.

Inside the country, one of the problems police face when trying to stop the heroin business is that drug offenses are a victimless crime. In a typical crime like robbery, the victim reports the crime and helps prosecute the offender. When a person commits the crime of buying, selling, possessing, manufacturing, or transporting illicit drugs, there is no individual victim involved. So, to be able to prosecute, the police have to witness the crime personally, arrest the perpetrator, and assist in the prosecution. This requires a huge amount of police time and effort.

When the goal is to arrest the user, an intrusive method of detection is required. This is because heroin use is a "status crime," which means a user cannot be detected by his or her actions. In other words, heroin users are breaking the laws for what they are and not for what they do.

In 1986, President Reagan passed the Drug-Free Workplace Act, making it legal to ask employees to give a sample of urine for drug detection. The method is still both controversial and inaccurate; after all, a urine test does not detect heroin after two days have passed since its use.

Also under the Reagan administration, the Fourth Amendment of the Constitution was altered. Until then, any evidence obtained as a result of an illegal search was inadmissible in court. Many times, a drug dealer was set free, even if found carrying drugs, because the police had arrested him or her without a probable cause to search in the first place. Under the new law, a police officer can obtain a warrant under false pretenses. If drugs are found during the search and the police claim to have acted in good faith, the evidence is accepted in court.

Other methods of law enforcement to stop drug use include posting cops on corners to scare off drug dealers, as Philadelphia Mayor John Street did in the summer of 2002 and the police sweeps in New York City that Mayor Rudy Giuliani started in 1993.

In a police sweep, a city block is closed, and everyone who happens to be there at the time is checked. Those found carrying drugs or without proper identification are arrested. Even though legitimate arrests are made this way, many complain that these methods are both expensive and intrusive into the liberties of normal citizens.

PENALTIES

Penalties against possession of a drug should not be more damaging to an individual than the use of the drug itself.

Jimmy Carter, 1977

The Boggs-Daniel Bill

POSSESSORS	MAXIMUM FINE	MINIMUM JAIL TERM	MAXIMUM JAIL TERM	PROBATION / PAROLE / SUSPENDED SENTENCE
1st offense	$20,000	2 years	10 years	permitted
2nd offense	$20,000	5 years	20 years	forbidden
3rd & subsequent	$20,000	10 years	40 years	forbidden

TRAFFICKERS (General)	MAXIMUM FINE	MINIMUM JAIL TERM	MAXIMUM JAIL TERM	PROBATION / PAROLE / SUSPENDED SENTENCE
1st offense	$20,000	5 years	20 years	forbidden
2nd & subsequent	$20,000	10 years	40 years	forbidden

The Boggs-Daniel Act of 1956 set sentencing guidelines for drug offenses. Anti-drug legislation like this was consolidated in Nixon's Comprehensive Drug Abuse Prevention and Control Act of 1970, which also established the schedules for illicit drugs that are still used today.

The origin of American drug law is the Harrison Narcotics Act, passed in 1914 by Congress to ensure record keeping of drugs and to unify the different state laws that regulated drug sales. But in 1919, the Supreme Court, by a narrow 5-4 decision held that the law's wording "prescribed in good faith" could not be used by doctors to dispense prescription drugs to reduce symptoms of narcotic withdrawal, thus inaugurating the Drug Prohibition era in which we still live.

Although President Nixon (1969–1974) is usually credited with starting the campaign against illegal drugs, several laws had already been passed during the 1950s that established minimum and maximum sentences for drug violations.

During the 1960s, the first baby boomers—those born between 1946 and 1958—came of age. A big proportion of this generation started to use drugs and challenged the traditional values of society. It was in this era that Nixon became president.

For Nixon, rising marijuana and heroin use was at the root of all American ills of the 1960s—rampant property crime, student and racial unrest, protests against the Vietnam War. In a significant departure from the country's philosophy then, he announced, "The country should stop looking for root causes of crime and put its money instead into increasing the number of police." So, for the first time the blame was shifted from society and put on the individual.

Nixon expanded the federal government's involvement in drug policy. He signed the Comprehensive Drug Abuse Prevention and Control Act of 1970, which consolidated prior anti-drug legislation and established schedules of illicit drugs. This act eliminated mandatory sentences for first-time offenders and reduced the penalty from possession of a controlled substance to up to one year in jail and a fine of up to $5,000. It also increased the maximum penalties for "professional criminal trafficking" in drugs to a $100,000 fine and a mandatory 10-year sentence for first-time offenders.

Nixon also authorized "no-knock" search warrants. Police could break doors and enter the suspect's property unannounced. Despite his tough measures and an increase in the annual budget for demand reduction (treatment/prevention strategies) from $59 million to $642 million, heroin use increased during the Nixon administration.

For a brief time, during President Ford's and President Carter's administrations, the role of environmental causes

MANDATORY SENTENCES

Many drug offenses carry mandatory sentences. A set formula predetermines the penalty before the crime is even committed. Some crimes have fixed penalties, such as life in prison or death. Other penalties, called minimum mandatory sentences, establish a minimum punishment for a given offense. Minimum mandatory sentences may be a five-year prison term for selling more than four ounces of heroin or a three-year term for selling heroin within 1,000 feet of a school.

The circumstances of each particular crime are left out of the mandatory sentence equation. Was the offender a follower or a ringleader? Was the offender a lifetime criminal or a first-time offender? Was the motivation greed or poverty? Was the dealer a professional drug leader or raising money to support a drug habit? How much drug was the offender dealing? These questions are irrelevant with mandatory sentences.

Although most judges agree that some crimes deserve tough penalties, many complain that mandatory sentences tie their hands and force them to give harsher sentences than they consider appropriate for the case.

for the drug problem was considered again. There were even talks regarding the legalization of certain drugs. When Ronald Reagan became president in 1981, all these efforts were halted, and the approach to drug control shifted once more toward tougher law-enforcement policies.

President Reagan was the first to officially declare a "war on drugs." According to Reagan, social conditions such as poverty were not to blame for crime and drug abuse, the individual was. He claimed that "right and wrong do matter, that individuals are responsible for their actions, that evil is frequently a conscious choice, and that retribution must be swift and true."

During the 1980s, U.S. policy took a position of "zero tolerance" toward drug addiction, including recreational drug use. Funding shifted accordingly from a balance between demand reduction (treatment/prevention) and supply reduction (enforcement) to one primarily focusing on enforcement.

According to *The Encyclopedia of Drugs, Alcohol, and Addictive Behavior*:

> The total federal budget for all demand-side and supply-control activities was about $1.5 billion in 1981, with about two-thirds allocated to law enforcement and supply control. . . . By 1989, the total had reached $6.7 billion, with two-thirds allocated to controlling drug supply. The resources escalated still further during the Bush administration, reaching $12.2 billion in fiscal year 1993.

To implement this zero tolerance policy, tougher crime bills were passed, which included:

- The Comprehensive Crime Control Act of 1984, which increased bail amounts and lengths of sentences for drug offenders and allowed federal authority to take assets and investigate money laundering.

- The Anti-Drug Abuse Act of 1986, which increased federal drug penalties and ordered mandatory minimum sentences for simple possession of drugs. It also doubled the penalties for anyone who knowingly involved juveniles in any drug activity and mandatory life sentences for those convicted of conducting a continuing criminal enterprise.

- The Anti-Drug Abuse Act of 1986 also made it a federal offense to sell drugs within 1,000 feet of a school. The Anti-Drug Abuse Act of 1988 expanded the previous law to those convicted of selling drugs within 100 feet of playgrounds, parks, youth centers, swimming pools, and video arcades.

- The Crime Bill of 1994, which provided for capital punishment for some types of drug selling, and instituted "criminal enterprise" statutes that called for mandatory sentences of 20 years to life.

- The 1998 Higher Education Act, which delayed or denied young people the right to receive federal aid for college if they had been convicted of a state or federal drug offense.

THE CONTROVERSY OVER HEROIN LEGALIZATION

Since the 1980s, many people from very different backgrounds have criticized the government policy on drugs. They believe the present policy must be modified and drugs should be legalized not because they are good for the individual but because the current policy of zero tolerance is causing greater harm to society than the drugs themselves. According to them, the drug policy of the last decade has resulted in a sharp increase in crime, since drug-related crime is a direct consequence of the illegality of the drugs and not caused by the drugs themselves.

Barry McCaffrey (left), former Director of the Office of National Drug Control Policy, meets with DEA officials in a congressional hearing to debate the pros and cons of drug legalization and decriminalization. Supporters of drug legalization believe current U.S. drug laws create more problems then they solve; however, those who favor current laws believe they protect children and maintain overall public health.

Critics of current U.S. drug policy also believe that it has clogged the criminal justice system. As a direct result of the zero tolerance policy, arrests for drug offenses increased 25 percent between 1986 and 1991. Likewise, because of the mandatory sentences and the "three strikes and you're out" legislation, which mandates sentences of 25 years to life for third felonies, the number of inmates held in prisons on drug charges has more than tripled since the Reagan administration. In August 1996, there were 1,127,132 inmates in state prisons and 500,000 in local jails and federal institutions. This brings the number to more than 1.7 million. This is without counting the more than 600,000 people on parole, 3,000,000 on probation and the more than 60,000 in juvenile facilities. If the number of inmates continues to grow at the present rate, any newborn in 2002 will have a one in 20 chance of serving time in jail during his or her lifetime, one in four if the baby is an African American male.

As a consequence of the overcrowding of prisons, wardens are forced to release violent prisoners before they have finished their sentences to make room for nonviolent drug offenders. By law, all drug offenders must serve their sentence in full, whereas other criminals, such as bank robbers and rapists, do not.

To further the credibility of legalization stance, supporters also claim that U.S. drug policy results in a deterioration of public health. The illegality of hypodermic needles forces addicts to share them. This contributes to the spread of AIDS and other infectious diseases among the intravenous population and eventually to the whole society.

Many of those who favor drug legalization believe that current anti-drug laws erode civil liberties. Especially criticized are "no knock warrants," the laws that allow seizing the property of convicted dealers, and the ones that make blood and urine tests at work legal.

Finally, anti-drug policy critics argue that current laws reduce the availability of drug treatments by reducing the budgets for these treatments, whereas the budget for enforcement of the war on drugs has skyrocketed in the last decades.

On the other side of the issue, critics of the legalization perspective argue that legalization of drugs will increase use by increasing availability and reducing the legal consequences of drug use. This increase in drug use will have a detrimental effect on the health of the society. For instance, the numbers of IV drug users will increase the risk of spreading AIDS.

Critics of the legalization debate believe that condoning drug use will give the impression to young people that using drugs is not dangerous.

Many people do not agree that drugs should be legal. Some believe that the only way to stop people from using drugs is to pass tougher laws. Some of these "tougher" laws that have been proposed are:

- To impose a curfew on minors

- To call in the National Guard to checkpoint areas in major cities

- To seize property of those indicted for drug offenses before conviction

- To pressure landlords to evict accused dealers

- To strip-search travelers at the border

- To prosecute parents of teenage drug users

- To build a buried Berlin Wall-type structure along the U.S. border with Mexico

- To shoot down the planes of suspected drug smugglers

- To do drug testing in private firms

- To give the police ten percent of the money and property they seize from drug dealers

Other critics, although opposed to legalization, agree with some of the points made by the legalization proponents. They believe, for instance, that the existing drug policy should be modified. Specifically, critics favor an increase in treatment availability, education, and money allocated to improve the economic opportunities of minority groups who are at high risk of drug use.

After all, Judge James P. Gray reminds us,

> History has shown us that we can pass all the laws in the world. But as long as there is a demand for drugs, the demand will be met. Our criminal laws will always be trumped by the law of supply and demand, and addiction cannot be eliminated by fiat. . . . Open, truthful, and realistic education, instead of shallow gimmicks and punitive laws, is what is needed to change the hearts, mind, and actions of our people.

As the British historian Paul Johnson writes, "The art of politics is the ability to find not the perfect solution but the best solution in an imperfect world."

Bibliography

Boaz, David, Ed. *The Crisis in Drug Prohibition.* Washington, D.C.: CATO Institute, 1991.

Carson-DeWitt, M.D. Rosalyn. Editor. *Encyclopedia of Drugs, Alcohol & Addictive Behavior.* Second Edition. Macmillan Reference USA.

Check, William A. *AIDS.* Philadelphia: Chelsea House Publishers, 2001.

Charen, Mona. *Cultural Factors Contribute To Chemical Dependency in Chemical Dependency. Opposing View Points.* Opposing View Points Series. San Diego: Greenhaven Press, Inc., 1997.

Davis, Joel. *Endorphins. New Waves in Brain Chemistry.* New York: The Dial Press. Doubleday & Company, Inc., 1984.

Eldredge, Dirk Chase. *Ending the War in Drugs. A Solution For America.* New York: Bridge Works Publishing Company, 1998.

Epstein, Joan F. and Joseph C. Gfroerer. *Heroin Abuse in the United States.* OAS Working Paper, August 1997. *www.health.org/govpubs/Rpo919*

Falco, Mathea. *The Making of a Drug-Free America. Programs That Work.* New York: Times Books, 1992.

Fernandez, Humberto. *Heroin.* Center City, Minn.: Hazelden Publishing, 1998.

Gallagher, Jim. *Heroin. Junior Drug Awareness.* Philadelphia: Chelsea House Publishers, 1999.

Indiana Prevention Resource Center. Indiana University. *Heroin Chic.* *www.drugs.indiana.edu/prevention/heroin.html*

Longenecker, Gesine L. *How Drugs Work. Drug Abuse and the Human Body.* Emeryville, Cal.: Ziff-Davis Press, 1994.

Gray James P. *Why Our Drug Laws Have Failed and What We Can Do About It.* Philadelphia: Temple University Press, 2001.

Hell, Richard. "Sid and Nancy." *Spin.* Dec. 1986.

Hughes, Barbara. *Drug-related Diseases.* Franklin Watts. A First Book, 1987.

Maltby, J.R. "Sherlock Holmes and anaesthesia." *Can. J. Anaesth.* 1988, 35: 1, 58–62.

Massing, Michael. *The Fix.* New York: Simon and Schuster, 1998.

McKenry, Leda M. and Salerno, Evelyn. *Mosby's Pharmacology in Nursing.* Nineteenth Edition, 1995.

Metzger, Th. *The Birth of Heroin and the Demonization of the Dope Fiend.* Washington: Loompanics Unlimited, 1998.

Miller, Marc. "Fatal Addiction." *Mademoiselle*, November, 1991. Reprinted in *Drug Abuse, Opposing Viewpoints.* San Diego: Greenhaven Press, Inc., 1994.

Miller, Richard Lawrence. *The Case for Legalizing Drugs.* New York: Praeger, 1991.

The National Center on Addiction and Substance Abuse at Columbia University. *1998 CASA National Survey of Teens, Teachers and Principals.*

National Institutes of Health. National Institue of Drug Abuse. *MTF (Monitoring the Future) Survey.* University of Michigan's Institute for Social Research, 2001.

Oliver, Marilyn Tower. *Drugs. Should They Be Legalized? Issues in Focus.* N.J.: Enslow Publishers, Inc., 1996

Pownall, Mark. *Drugs the Complete Story. Heroin.* Il.: Heinemann Educational Books Ltd., 1991.

Rodgers, Joann Ellison. *Biological Factors contribute to Chemical Dependency* in *Chemical Dependency. Opposing View Points.* Opposing View Points Series. San Diego: Greenhaven Press, Inc., 1997. First published under the title "Addiction: A Whole New View" in *Psychology Today*, September/October 1994 Sussex Publishers, Inc.

U.S. Department of Health and Human Services. *Treatment of Adolescents With Substance Use Disorders,* 1999.

U.S. Department of Health and Human Services. *Treatment of Opiate Addiction with Methadone. A Counselor's Manual,* 1994.

U.S. Department of Health and Human Services, *Effectiveness of Substance Abuse Treatment,* white paper, September 1995.

Further Reading

Non-Fiction

Books

Boaz, David, Ed. *The Crisis in Drug Prohibition.* Washington, D.C.: CATO Institute, 1991.

Carson-DeWitt, M.D. Rosalyn. Editor. *Encyclopedia of Drugs, Alcohol & Addictive Behavior.* Second Edition. Macmillan Reference USA.

Check, William A. *AIDS.* Philadelphia: Chelsea House Publishers, 2001.

Charen, Mona. *Cultural Factors Contribute To Chemical Dependency in Chemical Dependency. Opposing View Points.* Opposing View Points Series. San Diego: Greenhaven Press, Inc., 1997.

Davis, Joel. *Endorphins. New Waves in Brain Chemistry.* New York: The Dial Press. Doubleday & Company, Inc., 1984.

Eldredge, Dirk Chase. *Ending the War in Drugs. A Solution For America.* New York: Bridge Works Publishing Company, 1998.

Epstein, Joan F., Gfroerer, Joseph C. *Heroin Abuse in the United States.* OAS Working Paper, August 1997.

Falco, Mathea. *The Making of a Drug-Free America. Programs That Work.* New York: Times Books, 1992.

Fernandez, Humberto. *Heroin.* Center City, Minn.: Hazelden Publishing, 1998.

Gray James P. *Why Our Drug Laws Have Failed and What We Can Do About It.* Temple University Press: Philadelphia, 2001.

Massing, Michael. *The Fix.* New York: Simon and Schuster, 1998.

Metzger, Thomas. *The Birth of Heroin and the Demonization of the Dope Fiend.* Washington: Loompanics Unlimited, 1998.

Miller, Marc. "Fatal Addiction." *Mademoiselle,* November, 1991. Reprinted in *Drug Abuse. Opposing Viewpoints.* San Diego: Greenhaven Press, Inc., 1994.

Miller, Richard Lawrence. *The Case for Legalizing Drugs.* New York: Praeger, 1991.

Oliver, Marilyn Tower. *Drugs. Should They Be Legalized?* Issues in Focus. N.J.: Enslow Publishers, Inc., 1996

Pownall, Mark. *Drugs the Complete Story. Heroin.* Il.: Heinemann Educational Books Ltd., 1991.

Websites

American Association for the Treatment of Opioid Dependence (AATOD)
www.americanmethadone.org

Narcotics Anonymous
www.na.org

National Center on Addiction and Substance Abuse at Columbia University
www.casacolumbia.org

National Clearinghouse for Alcohol and Drug Information (NCADI)
www.health.org

National Institute on Drug Abuse (NIDA)
www.drugabuse.gov, www.nida.nih.gov

National Institutes of Health
www.nih.gov

National Medical Library
www.nlm.nih.gov

National Youth Anti-Drug Media Campaign.
www.freevibe.com

SoberRecovery
www.soberrecovery.com

Substance Abuse and Mental Health Services Administration
www.samhsa.gov
www.findtreatment.samhsa.gov

U.S. Drug Enforcement Administration
www.dea.gov

White House Office of National Drug Control Policy
www.whitehousedrugpolicy.gov

Fiction

Books

Davies, Luke. *Candy*. Ballantine, 1998.

Gavin, James. *Deep in a Dream: The Long Night of Chet Baker*. A biography of Chet Baker. Knopf, 2002.

Moody, Bill. *Looking for Chet Baker*. Walker and Co., 2002.

Spinrad, Norman. *Child of Fortune*. Bantam Books, 1985

Movies

Trainspotting, Directed by Danny Boyle, 1995.

The Basketball Diaries, Directed by Scott Kalvert, 1995.

Pulp Fiction, Directed by Quentin Tarantino, 1994

Killing Zoe, Directed by Roger Avary, 1994.

My Own Private Idaho, Directed by Gus Van Sant, 1993.

Drugstore Cowboy, Directed by Gus Van Sant, 1988.

Sid and Nancy, Directed by Alex Cox, 1986.

Traffic, Directed by Steven Soderbergh, 2000.

Index

Index

Picture Credits

page:

14: © Bettmann/Corbis

21: Courtesy NIDA

25: Courtesy NIDA

33: Research Report, "Heroin Abuse and
Addiction," Courtesy NIDA

39: NHSDA 2001 report, Courtesy SAMHSA

45: DAWNreport, Courtesy NIDA

51: © S.I.N./Corbis

57: NHSDA 2001 report, Courtesy SAMHSA

61: AP/Partnership for a Drug Free America

67: Associated Press, AP

68: Associated Press, AP

80: Associated Press, AP

88: Associated Press, AP

About the Author

Carmen Ferreiro, Ph.D., a native of Spain, obtained her doctoral degree in biology from the Universidad Autónoma of Madrid, Spain. She worked as a researcher for over ten years in Spain and the University of California at Davis. She has published several papers in the biochemistry and molecular biology fields. Presently she lives in the United States as an independent writer and translator.

About the Editor

David J. Triggle is a University Professor and a Distinguished Professor in the School of Pharmacy and Pharmaceutical Sciences at the State University of New York at Buffalo. He studied in the United Kingdom and earned his B.Sc. degree in Chemistry from the University of Southampton and a Ph.D. degree in Chemistry at the University of Hull. Following post-doctoral work at the University of Ottawa in Canada and the University of London in the United Kingdom, he assumed a position at the School of Pharmacy at Buffalo. He served as Chairman of the Department of Biochemical Pharmacology from 1971 to 1985 and as Dean of the School of Pharmacy from 1985 to 1995. From 1995 to 2001, he served as the Dean of the Graduate School and as the University Provost from 2000 to 2001. He is the author of several books dealing with the chemical pharmacology of the autonomic nervous system and drug-receptor interactions, roughly four hundred scientific publications, and has delivered over one thousand lectures worldwide on his research.